PRAISE FOR *RAINY STREET STORIES*

"In John Davis' prologue to *Rainy Street Stories*, he says what he has written will "find fellow feeling with the film noir genre." That's the perfect description for this series of short reflections, more fully developed essays and poetry focused on the ambiguous profession of espionage. Davis says these narratives are simply reflections, but they're more than that – they are compelling and beautifully written. And as Davis promises, that feeling of film noir permeates this collection."-- Joey Kennedy, Pulitzer-Prize winner.

"John Davis, recently retired from Army Intelligence, provides us with the conundrum of America in the current world of terrorism and hidden wars. How do we maintain our freedoms as we change and adapt to the new realities of engagement? While he gives us some answers, he describes the choices that we must make through analogies that clearly make the decision much easier. As he tells us in his prologue, "Nowhere is there a free pass from choices of good and evil." It is as if he is alluding to the fact that it is not only Intelligence professionals, but all of us in a free America that must, on a daily basis, make a Hobson's choice from among more than two equally unpalatable alternatives."-- D. Clark MacPherson, *SoHo Journal*.

"Poet and counterspy John W. Davis has written a cache of messages about deceit and loyalty, evil and good, danger and safety in his new *Rainy Street Stories*. His collection strings essays and incidents with poetic impressions interspersed like clues leading down the narrow alley that skirts the border of promise and betrayal, protection and sabotage. The good guys look more like the bad guys – like "secret brothers," Davis puts it -- than anyone could have guessed. This unusual memoir reveals nothing and still tells everything about Davis' real-life career in Cold War espionage. With vignette tributes to heroes of resistance and musings on true patriotism, this book offers complex and compelling ... reading for the thoughtful American."-- Kay Campbell, *Huntsville Times* award winning journalist

"*Rainy Street Stories* is a riveting book that reflects not only how the intelligence community operates but also defines Mr. John Davis' character. Mr. Davis offers important insights into the historical as well as current challenges the Intelligence Community faces. The factual accounts cited in his book are a must read for all operational and analytical professionals serving in the intelligence community."--Louis J. Kubik – US Marine Corps Reserve, retired, Department of Defense Civilian Counterintelligence Officer with two separate tours with the CIA.

"This little book deserves to be read by many, in many different walks of life. *Rainy Street Stories* is a wonderful testimony to the crucial importance of truth, goodness and, yes, Grace, in keeping our all too human character from going badly, sometimes horrifically astray. John W. Davis' collection of short pieces is an unwavering affirmation of the enduring power of virtuous principles in this often cruel and cynical world. Truly, it deserves to be read by many and its lessons taken deeply to heart."--Gray Sutherland, author, poet and translator.

"John W. Davis' *Rainy Street Stories* is a remarkable collection of vignettes, poems, short essays, prayers, and reflections that like gaslights in the fog help us glimpse the spectral outlines of a shattered world. That shattered world is our world, or the world we once believed we lived in, a world of goodness and moral coherence, but which has been turned by our own greed and violence into a killing field. *Rainy Street Stories* captures perfectly the confusion and ambiguity of this broken world, and the devious ways good people must master in order to function in it. But *Rainy Street Stories* also arouses hope that the broken pieces are not scattered beyond recovery, but are waiting for our commitment to reintegrate them into a whole fully lit by our passion for truth and the common good."--Rev. Mr. George Dardess, PhD., former professor of English, Tufts University and author of *Meeting Islam, A Guide For Christians.*

RAINY STREET STORIES

John W. Davis

For Sam,
A good man I'm
honored to call my
friend!
John W. Davis
HUNTSVILLE, AL
18 Jan 2014

RAINY STREET STORIES

John W. Davis

Rainy Street Stories

Published by: Red Bike Publishing

Copyright © 2013 by John W. Davis, Athens, Alabama

Published in the United States of America

www.redbikepublishing.com

Red Bike Publishing also publishes books in electronic format. Some publications appearing in print may not be available in electronic book format.

Library of Congress Control Number: 2013941654

ISBN: 978-1-936800-10-0

ABOUT THE AUTHOR

John William Davis is a graduate of Washington University in St. Louis, Missouri, his hometown. He is a retired Army officer and federal civil servant whose life's travels brought him into contact with a host of different people in the most unlikely of circumstances. A linguist, former combat arms and counterintelligence officer, he is an observer of the world, the better to try to understand. He lives with his wife Jane in Athens, Alabama, near his three grown sons.

To find out more about him, visit: www.redbikepublishing.com

ABOUT RED BIKE PUBLISHING...

Mission:

Red Bike Publishing exists to create value for our partners, shareholders and customers by building a business to last. As the foremost niche publishing organization, we offer what other publishers cannot; focused delivery of industry publications to enhance the professional's skill level. We do this by writing and publishing superior nonfiction, traditional and eBooks and providing empowering training resources at affordable prices.

VISION:

Red Bike Publishing will be valued for its one of a kind niche publishing and ability to positively impact our customers.

See more at www.redbikepublishing.com

DEDICATION

Dedicated to Marie Georges Picquart, (Strasbourg, September 1854-Amiens, 18 January 1914) French counterintelligence officer who did right, at great personal cost, for love of justice and truth.

"The wicked are always surprised to find that the good can be clever." Luc de Clapiers, Marquis de Vauvenargues (6 August 1715 – 28 May 1747) French writer.

"If only there were evil people somewhere insidiously committing evil deeds, and it were necessary only to separate them from the rest of us and destroy them. But the line dividing good and evil cuts through the heart of every human being, and who is willing to destroy his own heart?" Alexander Solzhenitsyn, author, *The Gulag Archipelago*

ACKNOWLEDGEMENTS

My thanks to friends and colleagues who offered valuable advice and helpful criticism. Thanks especially to those whose stories I tell here, for their honest reflections and confidence in me. These are the men and women who try to the best of their abilities, by the illumination they are given in the secret world, to do right for what they believe in. My heartfelt thanks as well to those caught up in our modern wars, whose stories tell of lives lived in sometimes horrific circumstances. Your stories need to be told to a world too often jaded. You show there is a golden spark to mankind. I offer heartfelt appreciation to those whose names are unknown to me, but who spoke with intense honesty in forms of revelation, and sometimes confession. My appreciation, too, to my publisher, Jeff Bennett, whose guidance is remarkable. My love and gratitude to my sons Marty, Will, and Kenny Davis who appear in several of these stories, but who really feature as inspiration for this book. A special thanks for Marty and his wife Terri for the outstanding artwork. Particular thanks for the encouragement of Debbie D'Ambrosio, Bill Hunt, Leo Sassen, Donald Clark MacPherson, publisher of the *SoHo Journal*, and my dad, Bill Davis, who all had faith in my work. Thanks, too, to the *Birmingham News, SoHo Journal, Decatur Daily, Huntsville Times*, and the *US Army Command and General Staff College's Military Review* where some of these essays first appeared. My greatest appreciation, however, is to my wife Jane. She encouraged me throughout, cared and offered attention, and much valued applied recommendations. Most especially she gave unqualified friendship, patient love, and a recognized joy of life which carried us through all our adventures together.

Artwork: Cover: Rainy Street, Berlin. Pen and Ink on Paper. Marty Davis

Cover photography: Terri Davis

PROLOGUE

Dear Reader,
Let me caution you. As you read these reflections about the secret world of espionage, counterintelligence, war, and terrorism, know beforehand that this is in great part a world of ambiguity. You must be satisfied that people and events may often remain a mystery. Not completely, however. Some of what you read here is as old and clear as ancient proverbs, even though practiced in the secret world. Nowhere is there a free pass from choices of good and evil. I hope thereby to help you appreciate somewhat the atmosphere of such a life, a life in the secret world.

My generation was greatly impacted by our parents' Second World War. We inherited the panoply of modern horrors which evolved thereafter. Ours was the Cold War, and its attendant culture of secrecy. We were at war with the Staatssicherheit, the "Stasi", the East German secret service, not to mention the Soviet KGB, "East Bloc" spies, and a host of others. Then came the carnivals of blood left in the Cold War's wake. Terrorist plots and actions in a variety of forms blossomed like poison plants and weeds from revolutionaries, insurgents, and wirepullers. There were clandestine wars in conjunction with Vietnam, Bosnia-Herzegovina, Northern Ireland, and in the Middle East, which were for the most part never declared. They happened as if they were always lying dormant, simply awaiting their murderous stage call.

Even during periods of apparent peace, such wars continue. I hope to explain what must of its nature remain largely tentative and opaque. We who dealt with this world saw only dimly, as through a glass darkly. Perhaps this is the best I'll be able to provide. Or perhaps more, that is for you to decide. We and our Allies fought for a free and open society, and like the Resistance personnel of the Second World War, hoped for a better world as a result. I believe this is what motivated many of my colleagues who were upright men and women, even when no one was watching. We fought for liberty and justice for all. In humility, I offer no 'solutions', only the thought that no cause is worth the loss of one's soul.

All the events I reflect upon here had some influential bearing on my life. Some are arguably best said in essay format. I relate also observations about events, people I met and their stories, artistic impressions, or readings which impacted my thinking. Others are thematic articles about some aspect of the secret world of intelligence, illusion, war, and security. I also offer poetic interpretations which attempt to capture some of the emotional and mental effects on those engaged in, or affected by, this strange world. Often the tentative grasp of a verse suggests more truth than volumes of prose.

You'll notice that these rainy street stories find fellow feeling with the film noir genre. Such films attempt to portray the opaque, mysterious, and inexplicable by use of the rainy street metaphor; for such has no clear delineations. Fog and mist literally embrace people, who try to see, but either due to some form of blindness cannot, or will not. This book attempts to help you see. Take your time as you read what is here. Nothing is as it seems, is it?

Darkness and an intangible sense of gloom or dread envelop the central battlefields of our world's secret wars. Such a world exists in parallel with that of normal life. It is a chameleon world, for it attempts to appear to belong to the everyday events happening around it, but does not. The surveillant wants to appear a part of a normal scene, but is not. We are confronted with the effects of these secret, real wars on real people, on real families, not least of all my own. I hope these appreciations of this world may cause you, too, to wonder about them as well. After all, as Leon Trotsky said, "You may not be interested in war, but war is interested in you."

If you remember only this, it will suffice. In war, there are no unwounded soldiers. Jose Narosky, the writer who said this, grew up in a Fascist dictatorship; he never saw a shot fired. He knew, however, that those fighting, especially those fighting in secret, or victims of such battles, are engaged in something which will not leave them unwounded. I hope this book will help explain why there are such casualties, especially in undeclared, unseen, secret wars. All the victims of these secret wars were not soldiers; indeed the majority are rightly called victims.

An ancient Chinese proverb says that the best way to find your way along an unknown road is to ask someone coming from the opposite direction. He can tell you how to prepare, what to be aware of, who you can trust, and signposts to watch for. You must then discern whether his advice is good or bad, true or false, and act accordingly.
I'm returning from a road into a secret world. I will be your Virgil on this walk along rainy streets. It is up to you to discern whether what you hear is true, or good, or not.

John W. Davis
Athens, Alabama
June 2013

TABLE OF CONTENTS

EDUCATION FOR LIFE

Arrayed for instruction, the six hostages were lined up against the nearest wall.

Passersby were blocked off, then drawn around, that they might see and be warned by what would happen next.

Some wondered who the grey men were, older of course, since the young had been long since been rounded up for forced labor.

Why chosen?

No reason, really, other than that something needed to be done, and these were the ones unlucky enough to be caught.

Like the strangest catch of all which happened the year before at the Bioscope movie house, where the film ended when the Gestapo surrounded the place and placed everyone under arrest.

In a short time, the old men were machine gunned.

One of the witnesses was a mother who pulled her daughter into a recessed doorway in hopes of protecting her.

But the little girl remembered the lesson, for life. She pointed out to her horrified mother there was one man standing at the wall for each year of her age.

POLAND'S FATE

Geniality came across with his every story. The old Polish guide in his faded uniform was delighted to describe the museum's stranger exhibits.

Papier mache scenes of rooms, filled with detailed, uniformed figures shot to pieces by resisters showed how the Polish secret army did in one Nazi officer or Wehrmacht squad after another.

Tiny bullet holes burned in the doll house sized walls showed the maker knew how automatic weapons impacted.

Easy enough to understand, I thought, since his only common language with me was a strange, hybrid German.

His was a German language learned, where?

"I was captured after the Warsaw uprising, together with my mommy," he inexplicably, disconcertingly, said.

Ah, I later deduced; he was no more than a child then, but could throw a Molotov cocktail. His foreign language skills didn't grow much in prison. He was a German speaker forever 12 years old.

"Then the Russians came. The Russians put me in jail, too. The Germans had already killed my mommy."

It is hard to see an old soldier's tears.

HUNTING NATHAN HALE

What if every country has a Nathan Hale?

His only regret was he had but one life to give for his country; but which country?

When the British hung him, did Colonials in America cease spying?

As he climbed the ladder, and the noose was fitted round his head, did he fear his cause was unjust?

Not the cause, just the unnatural loss of waking into the land of the living, I'd guess.

We believe he lives on, because he was one of ours.

In ballads, song, and verse, in history books, in tablets and shrines.

Hale is our hero, who did it for love.

No matter, we have to chase their Nathan Hales.

THE WHITE ROSE

The White Rose was the clandestine name of a tiny group of university German students and teachers who resisted Hitler.

Organized by Sophie and Hans Scholl, sister and brother, this naïve but idealistic group secretly printed and distributed leaflets around Munich, Germany in late 1942 denouncing Hitler's war. They wrote, "Everywhere and at all times of greatest trial men have appeared, prophets and saints who have cherished their freedom, who preached the one God and with His help brought the people to a reversal of their downward course. Man is free, to be sure, but without the true God he is defenseless against the principle of evil…"

Arrested shortly after their flyers appeared, they were convicted and executed along with several of their colleagues in 1943.

ONLY A FEW

The White Rose leaves only a shadow against the wall.

Nevertheless, the shadow appears to guide the light which comes after it.

Carefully notice that the wall diminishes wherever the rose's shadow has caused color to emerge.

Who knows today what light was shed by the unsophisticated few who made up the White Rose?

We know they spread their light far beyond their meager attempts; we remember them this very moment.

REMEMBER Z-1557 AND MAKE SURE IT NEVER HAPPENS AGAIN

While vacationing last summer my wife Jane and I decided to visit Flossenburg, Germany. This charming little town is nestled in among rolling hills, fresh brooks and quaint farmhouses. In the late 1930s, though, the Nazis chose Flossenburg as the site of a concentration camp. It was for that reason we drove along a particularly pleasant road in search of this place.

The West German town is, from all outward appearances, wholesome, sturdy and solid. It was difficult to find the old camp. We finally asked a pedestrian where the former concentration camp was and he indicated it was within a glade on the way out of town. We drove there and parked in a shaded lot. A guided path led us along memorials to the thousands of Europeans murdered there. Indeed, the actual incinerator was still in place. The strange feelings that overcame us were difficult to get a handle on.

The symbolic crosses and memorial tablets were fitting. Fitting is the appropriate word. Not moving. Not horrifying. A few flowers, recently placed, were what moved us. They were, in this park-like setting, perhaps the only scene that associated the place with the dread and terror of those many years ago. Real people, just like us, were rounded up, beaten, whipped, hung, shot and hacked to death there. Yet there was no sense any of that had happened. Except, of course, the anonymous people who placed the flowers. They had lost someone, felt the loss.

One of the last stops at Flossenburg is a re-created barracks building. Inside is a museum. Chilling, that. Scenes in black and white somehow make it all seem distant, and unreal. We noticed a marker dedicated to the famous inmates killed there – Canaris, Bonhoffer, Oster. And then we turned to go.

A couple who had arrived when we did was leaving the museum. I asked directions to another town and the man asked me what I thought of the memorial. I told him I really had gotten no sense of the place.

"No," he said in German. "It is like a park. We were recently in Auschwitz. I can tell you that as a retired engineer, with one company of engineering soldiers I could have Auschwitz fully operational in eight days."

Yet at Flossenburg, I said, there didn't seem to be any sense of what it had really been like.

"Nor for us," he said. "My wife could not even recognize the place when we drove in. You see, she was an inmate here."

It was then that I noticed the woman. She was small and very thin. I asked how she came to be put there. "Racial hatred," she said. "I was a gypsy, living in Danzig. In 1941 my entire family was rounded up. We were put into cargo trains and brought to Auschwitz, where they kept us crammed like animals in a barracks for five months."

She pulled up her sleeve, revealing the tattoo – Z-1557. Z for *Zigeuner*, or gypsy. "Then, one day, they had a formation to select women who could work. I was chosen and sent at 3 o'clock by train to Ravensbrück, a concentration camp for women. I learned years later, due to the remarkable records that the Nazis kept that my family together with all the gypsies then held in Auschwitz were massacred at 7 o'clock that very evening."

My wife and I were stunned. We'd never met an actual inmate of such a place. We didn't know what to say.

She finished her story. "After being held in Ravensbrück, I was sent to Buchenwald, and after that to this place."

"Did you see the photographs inside?" her husband asked. "Did you see the one where the commandant and guards of Flossenburg were being tried?"

I recalled a photograph that showed about 30 German prisoners being tried by an American tribunal. "Did you see the look on the Germans' faces? They looked like bored opera viewers. Only 17 of those tried received the death penalty, three times that number were free men within eight years. They really did escape from justice. I think that the whole lot of them should have been finished off," he said.

"We visited all the places where my wife was once held. She could not bring herself to go into Auschwitz," he said.

That camp, in Poland, and some others – Buchenwald, in what was East Germany, for another – seem more as they might have been when in use. Not Flossenburg.

"This place is a park. Who can even tell that there was a camp here?" the man said. "I think that here in the West the memory of such a place will go away in another generation."

The tears his wife cried that day were for the murdered who were still part of her life after all these years. Can we imagine ourselves there? Can we imagine our own families in such a place?

Such places as Flossenburg were huge operations during the war. They were immense and readily visible from afar. Whether those who were alive then knew is a question for the past. Whether those of us alive today remember and do all in our power to stop such things from ever happening again is a question that we must answer for.

It has been said that to do good and avoid evil is not enough. We have to do good and undo evil.

I think the sensation I had at Flossenburg was an awareness of evil.

26

That evil was present. It was smug because it was waiting. Waiting for us to forget in the park that is Flossenburg now.

CONFESSION, BERLIN, 1981

This street is my secret cathedral; its apartment blocks the rows of saints on either side. They stand silent sentinels under moonlight; only raindrops mumble orations on street and rooftops.

Street lamps waver in the mist. No acolyte makes a move. It is quiet here, but for the prayer on my umbrella. Ahead, only a gloomy green glow lights where the altar should be: a marquee over a theater at the end of the block.

I make the sign of a cross on the street lamp at the corner, which my unknown recipient will see and keep walking.

He comes to make confession, but we cannot meet here. Not now.

I am the priest of this secret cathedral, and we will meet a half hour from now, but not at this lamp. He knows that.

I walk a directionless oratory in case adversaries of my secret confessional are watching. They are always watching, we are taught to believe.

In time he passes under the marquee, and pauses in odd genuflection. I wait for him there.

"It always rains in Prague on a Saturday night," he says as if in private prayer, his eyes hidden under an umbrella and hat. He looks away, as if to God out there.

"Stay here out of the rain. The bus doesn't come for another fifteen minutes, if you are looking for it," I comment, to let him know we are alone in this strange confessional.

28

"No, I only have a short walk," he responds to my invocation.

Our opening prayer concluded, I am sure he is my expected one. We stand side by side. He speaks. I listen and nod. The confession over, I stand alone as he makes his recessional into the fog.

LANGUAGE AND PROPAGANDA

Ohne Juda, ohne Rom, wird gebaut Germanien's Dom! Heil! -- With-
out Jews, without Rome, we shall build Germany's cathedral! Heil!
--Adolf Hitler, traditional conclusion to speeches, Men's Asylum,
Vienna, Austria, 1910-1913

T he modern viewer observes the Hermann O. Hoyer painting, "In the Beginning Was the Word" with nothing less than
shock. What is so shocking about a dark picture that represents
a man speaking to a small, attentive audience in a Gasthaus? Perhaps
the image of Adolf Hitler, dressed in benign civilian attire as he ad-
dresses a diverse gathering of Germans, conveys a specific blasphemy.
The title of the artwork, after all, alludes to the opening verse of John's
Gospel. Perhaps the direct parallel of Hitler's arms, bent in mirror image of the Nazi swastika on the flag which hangs directly behind him,
conveys a subtle image of the crucified Christ. Maybe it is the trans-
fixed attention of the listeners who are enlightened, both literally by
the only ambient light depicted in the painting, and symbolically, by
the message of the speaker from whom the light seems to issue.

Since the painting was made in depression era Germany, the contem-
porary viewer would immediately, even unconsciously, infuse a lifetime of learned Christian symbolism to the rendering. Here was the
savior bearing a message of hope in those dark days of inflation, unemployment, and social chaos. He was the new Messiah, this Adolf Hitler. The artist wanted to show that Hitler was the redeemer of fallen
Germany, the savior who would liberate them from the evil Versailles
Treaty brought about by the lies and betrayals of the satanic Jews, none
of whom is visible in this picture. Indeed, the mysterious origin of the
painting's light over the listeners suggests Pentecost. That is the moment traditionally portrayed by symbolic 'flames of enlightenment', as

if to show the truth of Christ shining on the apostles, who then went forth to spread the word. The listeners in the painting would be so enlightened and spread Hitler's new truth.

The Nazi genius for propaganda allowed them to shamelessly usurp for their own ends symbols and terminology found in the Jewish and Christian writings of Tanak and New Testament. These symbols and words were ingrained in a German population through years of religious instruction, literary usage, and social convention. Even a secular German could not escape a language suffused with originally religious terminology.

This essay will consider Nazi usage and the context in which it flourished. I will demonstrate how one German-American Catholic priest, Monsignor Martin Hellriegel, in the spirit of a Papal encyclical of the time, countered such manipulation with truth, and brought back honest usage to words shamelessly exploited by the neo-pagans. Hellriegel saw in Nazi blasphemy the insidious twisting of the meaning of words which, Pied Piper like, led the listener away from the truth and into a dark forest of confusion and evil.

Adolf Hitler saw the world with a distinctly 'religious' viewpoint. That is to say his world view was clearly bound up in a fall from grace, resurrection, and victory schematic. He specifically introduced this idea in *Mein Kampf,* and restated it in virtually every public utterance thereafter.

In the beginning was the Edenic German past, the great victorious Reich of Franco-Prussian War days. Was it not thunderous German cannon and proud soldiery which brought about this triumphal era? The wholesome Germanic stock prevailed in a sort of Darwinian triumph against lesser Europeans. This past was further characterized by a virtuous Germanic racial pride, a *Völkisch* culture of simple honesty, hard work, communal integrity and physical wholesomeness.

Into this Eden came the evil serpent; into Eden came the Jew. Attached to the integrated Völkisch host, the parasitical Jew leeched it of life. The Jew attained inclusion not through virtuous action and social harmony. Rather by blandishment, money, and exploitation of human frailty he affixed himself to the living body of the German people. The Jew, as characterized by his Talmudic philosophy, created a false trope to protect himself from expulsion from the alien body, the concept that the weakest must be protected. He spread his false doctrine through the liberal press, his servile politicians, and his religion. His philosophy was 'unnatural' for it flew in the face of simple biology. To suggest that human dignity was not manifested in the triumph of the strong, (as proven by the victorious 1870 Reich), but rather in how the strong treated the weakest among them, was an insidious means of debilitating the otherwise powerful German race. 'To protect the weak, the outsider,' was a lie that could be traced back even to its cunning insinuation into the Christian concept of the Beatitudes or the Good Samaritan. How to expose this racial cancer, this contagious tuberculosis injected into Germanic culture? Consider, Hitler argued, what this cancer had already done.

The young Hitler, after some three years on World War I front lines, wounded in the face by shrapnel, felled by a bullet to the thigh, and gassed by Allied chlorine bombs, recovered near wartime Berlin. During recuperation he traveled there to find it a nest of complaints and defeatism. This attitude prevailed even though Russia had collapsed in revolution and the French were in disarray. As Hitler later wrote it was obvious why Germany lost the war which by all observable accounts it was winning. Germany was betrayed. The November criminals sabotaged Germany and so stabbed the Fatherland in the back. They did so in thousands of cowardly ways. Their Marxist unions fought a common steadfastness on the home front. The inconstant Churches subverted the war effort by religious softness, while the worthless, lying politicians deceived the simple *Volk*. Behind them all was the wire pulling Jew. The Versailles Treaty brought them to power, a power totally unearned, totally corrupt, and totally alien to the German way.

The bourgeois liberals, the Marxists, and the Church, the Catholic

Church in particular, militated against the Germanic race. Each in its own way brought about Germany's downfall. Philosophically, they all sought universality and converts to party, class, or religion respectively. Conversely, one was born into the German *Herrenvolk*. In any case, each had in its way brought about the downfall of Germany. Hitler would save the Germanic race from the crest of oblivion to which it had been brought. He would do so by excising from the land that very parasite which brought it to this end, the Jew, the manipulator behind each of these entities.

So it was that Hitler applied one of the lessons he learned best in the trenches of Belgium: propaganda. He would co-opt the strengths of his enemies to his own ends.

Religious language suffused the Third Reich. The Nazis turned the benign concepts about God to their own ends by subtle means. They were wolves in sheep's clothing.

This distortion was exposed by the 1937 Vatican Encyclical, *Mit Brennender Sorge*, (With Burning Anxiety), uniquely published originally in the German language. It excoriated the consistent Nazi dismantling of the Concordat between Rome and Berlin. Not only had the Nazis broken virtually every component, among which were provisions for religious education, public practice of religion, and social activities, it had even begun to subvert the truths behind the language of the Christian religion.

Beware, Venerable Brethren, of that growing abuse, in speech as in writing, of the name of God as though it were a meaningless label, to be affixed to any creation, more or less arbitrary, of human speculation...Our God is the Personal God, supernatural,...who will not, and cannot, tolerate a rival God by His side. --Mit Brennender Sorge, Pius XI, Encyclical, 1937

The poison spread not only throughout Germany, but to Germans in America as well. The faux religion of Nazism, or at least the apparent acceptance of religion by the Hitler state, deceived millions. For example, by substituting apparently wholesome Hitler Youth activities for confirmation ceremonies, or inserting Nazi themes into prayers, or even creating national ceremonies to replace religious rituals, the cultural religiosity of the country was co-opted and believers duped into slowly accepting Nazi beliefs.

Let us examine one example of how this usurpation of language was identified, and how, in the spirit of *Mit Brennender Sorge*, it was countered in a most unlikely way. This example will demonstrate how the insidious influence of appropriated language was deftly and simply countered, so that Nazism's influence was blunted among German-Americans before our entry into the war.

In night's darkest hour every November 9th, to commemorate the Nazi *coupd'etat* of 1923, a mystical midnight oath-taking ceremony took place in a sacred hall under the eyes of Adolf Hitler. There the SS, Hitler's special troops, took an oath of personal loyalty to him. One remembers, " Splendid young men, serious of face, exemplary of bearing and turnout; an elite. Tears came to my eyes when, by the light of the torches, thousands of voices repeated the oath in chorus. It was like a prayer."

During their rise to power, the Nazis usurped virtually all traditions, symbols, and words of pious German Christianity. Indeed, the most egregious was to call Adolf Hitler the Savior. Perhaps this extract from the SS catechism characterizes this subtle transference best: The question, 'Whom must we primarily serve?' required the response, 'The people and our Führer, Adolf Hitler'. 'Why do we believe in Germany and the Führer?' ' Because we believe in God,...and in the Führer, Adolf Hitler, whom He has sent us." This echoes the first questions of the Christian catechism.

Indeed, by 1941 the Hitler's successes appeared Providential, as he claimed. He raised Germans from the shame of Depression joblessness and revived a beaten people's pride by giving them military victory. His rule extended to virtually every land and nation of Europe, North Africa, and Eurasia to Moscow. But in his dominion salvation required absolute obedience to Hitler's belief in racial supremacy and hatred of the 'race defilers', the Jews. Hitler's rule required a gradual but inevitable denial of a personal, loving God in favor of faith in racial victory.

Far away in little Baden, an American community settled by Germans on the banks of the Mississippi, a parish priest was composing a song that would strike the Nazis a blow from which they would never recover. Father Martin Hellriegel, a German immigrant and pastor to several communities in the St. Louis, Missouri area, considered the rise of racial nationalism in his former homeland. As Hellriegel read in the 1937 Papal Letter entitled, *With Burning Anxiety*, (the only encyclical written in the German language), the Pope outlined how Germans had lost their way. They had abandoned traditional Christianity in favor of a twisted racial Darwinism that called 'immortality' not survival of man after life on earth, but survival of the race; that maintained 'revelation' was not God's word to Man, but suggested the triumph of race and blood over lesser peoples. The Pope further noted that daring to suggest that even the greatest of men was on a par with Christ, our Savior from sin and death, would be to make the man a "Prophet of Nothingness."

Hellriegel knew his people. To defeat subtle Nazi usurpation of Christ's words and mission, he would restate the Christian message simply and clearly for all the world. The pastor knew what Christ intended when our "yes" should mean "yes, our "no mean "no". Hellriegel found an energetic, almost martial tune in an old copy of the Mainz (Germany) church music book. To the music from 1870, he wrote new lyrics. They are a point by point rebuttal of Nazi beliefs. He called the song "To Jesus Christ, Our Sovereign King" and he wrote it in 1941 at the height of Nazi power.

Hellriegel's opening salvo was that Jesus, not Hitler, was "...our Sovereign King, who is the World's Salvation". If Jesus was sovereign, Hitler was not. If, as the Catholic Church proclaimed, all in the world could be saved, no claim of racial peculiarity could stand. "All praise and homage do we bring, and thanks and adoration" was a direct slap at the obsequious accolades offered Hitler for having brought Germans back into wealth, prestige, and power.

It is the refrain, "Christ Jesus Victor, Christ Jesus Ruler, Christ Jesus Lord and Commander," which is the most powerful statement of faith. Hitler promised Sieg (victory), and was the Führer (ruler), who rescued Germany from the hydra-headed oppressions of the Versailles Treaty, the traitorous Jews, the internationalist Church and Communists. At the very height of German battlefield victories Hellriegel declared not Hitler but Christ as the true Commander. (In later years, that intentional military term was changed to 'redeemer'.) Hellriegel's refrain, repeated over and over again, specifically denied each of Hitler's claims, just as had been done in the Papal Letter.

Indeed, "Thy reign extend, oh King, benign, to every land and nation. For in thy Kingdom, Lord divine, alone we find salvation," contended that Christ's kingdom, not Hitler's empire, was where man would be saved. Even the very Hitler oath, required of every government and military official in Germany was specifically attacked in this song. Not loyalty to Hitler; not, as the Hitler oath claimed, "I swear to thee, and to the superiors whom thou shall appoint, obedience unto death. So help me God.", but rather as Hellriegel wrote, "To thee and to thy church great king, we pledge our hearts oblation, until before thy throne we sing, in endless jubilation."

The hymn "To Jesus Christ our Sovereign King" is sung even today. Hitler's claims lie long forgotten. The challenge this song threw at the apparent victor of Europe, at the height of his greatest power, was mighty. For, as each verse attested, there was a greater truth which stood in opposition to Hitlerism. There were other, more ancient meanings to the words usurped by the Nazis. Simple and clear, the hymn carried a power to change hearts by speaking the truth.

GOOD AGENT WORK

Dressed only to run, she burst into my office.

C'mon, I saw him! Saw who? The guy you read about yesterday! I ran right by his car on the compound and remembered the license plate you read to us yesterday!

Enthusiasm dissolves into intense action.

Calls; set up teams, contact MPs, counterparts, get cars ready, pistols holstered, coats, always coats for this country that knows no summer. A thousand questions unasked, unanswered, almost thought of, out the door.

Was it really that fast?

"Halt in the name of the law!" Did the biggest MP in the world really say that as he held a .45 on the stunned driver? Just like the movies.

Our agents.

INCIDENT

The rain against the windshield must have been reassuring; it happened even on the dullest of days.

The green and gray of the Dutch countryside, flat and unending, offered assurance.

We'd only heard the Germans were collegial, refined, even sportsman-like.

They and ours had become like secret brothers, so it appears.

They were desperate, we'd heard, hoping against hope we'd listen.

But we headquarters spies were cautious, far too cautious for those field men who judged us blind.

So despite our directive, they drove to that meeting at the border cafe.

Sitting in their Buick, it must have been warm, even reassuring.

Until the three black Mercedes blocked them in, and their brothers Cain appeared.

SERVING YOUR COUNTRY

My friend Tony joined the Peace Corps. His story puts flesh on the fashionable chatter these days about public service.

Tony wrote me one day to say that he'd dramatically changed his life. As a middle-aged human resource manager, he felt his civil-service position with the city of St. Louis was empty. His job was steady, well-paid, but rudderless.

The prospect of a career characterized by gray, endless bureaucratic duplicity and indifference left him in a sad funk. He said in his application to the Peace Corps, "I want work worth doing." Such an appeal was instantly accepted.

A motivated, educated and caring middle-aged volunteer comes too seldom into the Peace Corps. Soon Tony was outbound for training in the Fiji Islands.

Such change does not come without cost.

Tony sold his home, left his job, gave away his beloved dog and said farewell to his mother, brothers and sisters. Think about it - could any of us do this for the purpose of serving others?

Service today is spoken of as a sort of repayment for a university loan, for instance. Tony offered service to others as a service to this country. "I'm paying my debt to America," he said.

No one gave Tony anything to make this decision. He served overseas because he believed America had something to offer, because he felt he could be a good ambassador for his country.

The training in the tropics was hard, demanding he adapt to rural, rustic conditions. He dealt with a new land as an inhabitant, accepting no special treatment.

He became the best America could offer to others. He respected those on the tiny island on which he served. He joined in their Christian religious services and social activities. He was accepted by all as a good man who came to serve. Tony learned their ways as an equal.

He wrote of his experiences among the Fijians with incredible clarity and insight, publishing various articles on life there. What is more important, though, is that he engaged every farmer, fisherman, homemaker and civil servant he met in Lakemba, his little Fijian island, in discussions about that distant land America.

So what was, finally, served?

We Americans have come to believe, somehow, that our strength abroad is best represented by our ships of war, cruise missiles and ominous diplomatic "signals."

Ask yourself, did our forefathers respect the English army stationed in our cities and farmhouses in 1775? Or did they not rather respect the ancient rights of parliamentary democracy and civil justice which Thomas Jefferson wrote about in his Declaration of Independence? Tony learned that we are respected - admired, in fact - when we clearly demonstrate our belief in liberty. It was our liberty that fascinated the Fijians. As simple as that.

He realized that America is the dream of the world because here no one is a slave of his history, his race, his traditions, or his former culture. He is free to become someone else - an American. We are admired the world over because of our optimism that springs from our belief that we are free to constantly renew ourselves in the pursuit of happiness.

Tony renewed himself in Fiji. America is the better for it. In a thousand ways, his optimism and a joy of life made the little Fijian island of Lakemba forever a place where the idea of America is fondly remembered.

SPY CONFERENCE?

Whoever heard of a 'Spy Conference'? Aren't those meetings supposed to happen on darkened, rainy street corners? Aren't the participants forbidden to use their real names, and make contacts which last only long enough to pass along secret, coded messages? No film noir has a moment where participants break character, the film stops, and actors mingle to discuss fantastic escapes, stolen documents, or lost persons...do they? What would a visitor to a 'Spy Conference' expect to find there, anyway? More intriguing, who would go to such a conference?

Just such a conference exists. Indeed so far as I can make out, it occurs only once a year for the general public. The "Raleigh Spy Conference" happens each year. It is the imaginative creation of Mr. Bernie Reeves, the editor and publisher of the hip, but professional and thoughtful current events, politics, and arts Metro Magazine of Raleigh, North Carolina. Its remit is "From the Triangle to the Coast," and it covers everything from architecture to zoology (there is a great natural history museum in Raleigh) with equal gusto.

Reeves, through a host of chance encounters turned opportunities, met and befriended several former CIA professionals. As a man who can be counted on to win a friend, he came up with an idea to introduce to the general American public an often vilified and little understood part of our society, the secret world of spy and counterspy. After all, we spend billions on the subject, so why not try to learn what really happens in that business?

Or can we? Do we have a 'need to know'? Reeves is quick to point out that secrecy, and the need to know, are still hallmarks of the espionage world. Yet, in the interest of history, or context, or to make available to a free and democratic people the fruits of efforts done on their behalf by elected governments, information from this twilight world has become more and more available thorough declassification and publication.

I spoke with a team from the CIA. Yes, that Central Intelligence Agency! They were at the conference to present a tale of daring do which matches any novel or fantasy writer's most imaginative effort. We heard of a deception operation which recovered a cask of clandestinely taken photographs from the ocean floor, having been accidentally dropped there from a camera in outer space. Most of those I spoke to were amazed at this revelation, but even more at the technological lengths required to do the job. What's more, outside in the common area after the slide presentation there were documents offered free of charge to the public, written by experts from the CIA on this and other subjects. It was as if someone with the price of admission would drop into the KGB headquarters and pick up documents, there for the taking. At this spy conference, actual declassified formerly secret documents were handed out in thematic booklet format, so that the public could read about what our country did to keep the peace.

Because what was required in the secret world over the past decades to keep the peace is what such a conference is all about. No, this is not some government policy paper hand out. For the conference is much more than that. While I listened intently to an FBI historian give an overview of the role of J. Edgar Hoover after his era is gone, I heard as well from a journalist whose methodical, fact checking expertise is unquestioned. His revelation was that the source for the Watergate revelations was not necessarily a whistle-blowing hero, but rather a focused promoter of his own personal agenda, which would be served if the FBI were shown in a bad light. After a careful presentation, one left this presentation wanting the book which substantiates the argument.

Of course, that is the additional value of such a conference. Many assertions are made, but few without controversy. I met at least two authors there, one of whom introduced himself as a free lancer, the other a writer of fiction. Both had grist for their mill at such a conference, because not only are the authors of the presentations available for discussions afterward, but remain for the entire three day conference. One can meet them casually at two events planned for such purposes, an opening reception and another after hours restaurant gathering. Without doubt, they are also available at your convenience as well.

The average person cannot imagine actually meeting some of the people who were spies; much less the scholars who sift, assess, and write about that shadowy world. Even less likely our average person would never, ever, expect to be able to ask such people about the reality of the goings on behind the Bay of Pigs, the Berlin Wall, what really happened at Dallas, or why Bin Laden escaped for so many years.

The masters of the trade come to this conference. Here one might meet Nigel West, formerly of the British Parliament now a world renowned intelligence scholar. Here you will meet also men of the caliber of Cambridge University's Christopher Andrew, who together with the KGB librarian who defected with thirty years of secret notes, wrote two books on this archive. What astounded me was how you can meet them as one would any expert, and find them willing to discuss the broadest, or most obscurantist questions.

One example was Brian Latell, whose expertise over decades of dealing with Cuba for the CIA is invaluable. I found him not only clear in his contention that Cuban intelligence is a far greater threat than one might imagine, but perfectly open about his handling of case officers, of declassified documents, and other sources of his thoughtful presentation.

I like it as well that the conference does not shy from controversy. As mentioned in passing by 'Bernie', as he is fondly known by regular attendees, for whom he is always available, the fate of Admiral Kimmel, who was blamed for the intelligence fiasco at Pearl Harbor, the misreading of intelligence before 9/11, and even the whole story of the man falsely accused and investigated before Bob Hanssen was revealed to be the spy for the Soviets, then Russians, are all on the table. Why there

44

is such a conference revealed itself to me more and more as the days passed.

I met people from many walks of life. Here was a sailor who took advantage of his merchant ship's docking in Charleston to see what this was about. Another writer spoke at some length of her experience in the area of fantasy novels, while another man was a pilot. There were students, one of whom was studying environmentalism. He was amazed to hear from an actual analyst how knowing weather was itself a major intelligence goal. A boat builder, a businessman, several former intelligence personnel from the 'beltway', a medical doctor, and a host of others characterized only a small segment of this crowd nearing 300. Each seemed to have a different interest in coming, but all were gratified that such a possibility existed, to learn and to see. (As an aside, a remarkable coincidence: The North Carolina History Museum is the venue for this conference. It has on permanent display formerly secret sabotage, communication, and coding devices donated by a former OSS officer from the Second World War. Also, this conference had a collector's special display of coding paraphernalia going back to the 1760's!).

It is because we are a free country, whose intelligence services are operated by men and women of dedication to this land. They are citizens just like you and me who operate within a system of laws that often are little known, or understood. Nevertheless, they are there to protect our nation just as any soldier, sailor or airman. Their story is often not known, because it should never be revealed if the secrets still serve a purpose. Yet now they can, in some cases, not only be known but celebrated, or learned from. Bernie Reeves and his team have done a great service to our nation, echoed by a comment made by one of the CIA public affairs persons. "We need to remain an open society, even though sometimes we need to work in secret." In a world beset by the age old question, "What is truth", such activities as the Spy Conference held in Raleigh, due to the vision of Bernie Reeves, some local friends, and some former intelligence people, we are a little closer to answering that question. A free nation must be open; its people must keep themselves informed, the better to preserve the peace. In time, all secrets become known. What a testimony to a free people that we can talk about, discuss, and learn from even those events which were once our only protection in a dangerous world. After all, Edmund Burke, that great English parliamentarian once said, "The best national defense is a good education."

HOLDING TOGETHER

I don't know if I was ready to come back to America. After 13 years abroad as a soldier and civil servant, I knew it would be difficult. The talk was of a new, multicultural America, a "pluralist" society. America is, after all, my homeland. I was born in Missouri. But my boys are all teenagers now. They grew up overseas. So, it was sure to be strange, this homecoming.

To ease the boys' return, they flew out to visit their Midwestern grandparents. That much of America was just as before, baseball games, barbecues and swimming. My wife and I said goodbye to the boys in New York, where we would await the arrival of our car by sea.

As we drove out of Bayonne, I could barely glimpse the Statue of Liberty, green against a gray sky. I imagined that maybe immigrants to Ellis Island could only see as much, and wondered as I did, what it all meant.

Our trip to our new home in Alabama would take us across the Middle Atlantic states. It was in Pennsylvania that I learned a haunting truth about America.

In Philadelphia, we visited Constitution Hall and the Liberty Bell. I tried to imagine the significance of what I saw. In that very hall Americans staked together their lives, fortunes and sacred honor on liberty. A young Czech student we met there commented that the American ideals of "life, liberty and the pursuit of happiness" made us what we are.

The men in Liberty Hall declared to the whole world that we are something new, Americans, not a collection of various colonists who happen to live in the same area.

Beyond Philadelphia, in the Pennsylvania countryside, Valley Forge sits in a placid park like setting, with tidy lawns and well-trimmed trees and bushes. There was nothing to make real the fact that hundreds of American soldiers froze and hungered in this very place for liberty. What did all these impressions mean?

It is strange that these sites are almost lost in the rush of our times. Liberty Hall is quaintly out of place, a small colonial building nestled amid titanic skyscrapers. Valley Forge could be a park.

A few miles away, however, the battlefield at Gettysburg was different. I stood toward twilight at a tree-line, about a mile or so from a ridge named after the old town cemetery. In 1863, Americans from Alabama stood in my place. Across the same open ground, other Americans from New York prepared to kill them. What brought these, my ancestral countrymen, to this ruthless finality historians call the field of Pickett's charge?

All of those men on that long ago day grew up in the same America, conceived in liberty. Yet they decided that something made them different, one from another. They believed that their regional characteristics took precedence over their common dream of life, liberty and the pursuit of happiness. Instead of Americans, they were Confederate-Americans and Union-Americans.

They were multicultural.

They would settle their differences by killing each other. And so the embattled farmers and workers did that July so long ago.

The American idea of *E Pluribus Unum*, out of many, one, was suspended during the brothers' war of 1861-65. Can *E Pluribus Unum* ever be reconciled with the alien notion of multiculturalism? My homecoming was haunted at that battlefield on that evening. Are we still one as a nation, although derived from many? Will we make the same terrible error that our forefathers made? Will we decide that our common dream of life, liberty and the pursuit of happiness is now only a dead, cold conceit of the past? Are we no longer one America, but many who happen to be in the same place? Is such a notion not exactly the opposite of those men who stood together in Liberty Hall? Do we not remember that a house divided against itself cannot stand?

I couldn't shake these ominous thoughts as we drove away from Gettysburg to our new home in this, my homeland.

THE LINE CROSSER

He wore a navy blue overcoat, and a black trilby hat like no one had seen in years.

A line crosser, his business kept him active, but his discretion kept him going.

Beers of the world never compared to his Pilsner back home, And he enjoyed every moment of laughter and stories with me.

Most important to him, was my friendship.

Most important to me, was whatever he needed from me, in return for what I received from him.

I kept him happy. He brought me the blue liquor Karlovy Vary was famous for.

I kept him from being lonely.

I kept him on the road.

DOWNSTAIRS

The basement bar was known to few.

Simple, someone even left a captured Hitler plaque on the wall.

Others from years gone by left other silent memorabilia.

Others passed along stories told through the years.

Chilly, if the door was not closed, of course, but camaraderie warmed the place quickly.

We felt at ease with each other, who knew one another's real stories, or at least what we believed were real.

The staircase led back to the secret world; not this, this could not be part of that world.

VETERAN'S DAY REFLECTION

Few know how to deal with another's sorrow. On a long ago autumn day, not unlike any other brisk day in late 1983, I received a call. My caller said a close mutual friend, Kevin, was believed killed in a shocking bombing in southern Beirut, Lebanon. Kevin was a Marine slain by a suicide bomber who drove a non-descript truck laden with the equivalent of six tons of explosives. Upon detonation, the Marines' quarters collapsed in a cloud of acrid smoke, fire, and mammoth blocks of rubble. 241 Marines died that day and many, many more were critically wounded, sent to hospitals across the region.

I remember Kevin every Autumn. He was a classmate of mine. Over a long military course we came to share stories, friendship, his great sense of humor and bonhomie. We all formed a fateful bond at that course, one that remains for a lifetime. After the class, we each went our separate ways, remaining in touch professionally or for personal reasons. Our conflicts in those days against terrorists, warlords, spies and dictators' whims were seldom newsworthy, though often fatal. There are enigmatic military memorials I've visited which indicate deaths occurred on a certain date, but no names are recorded. Like many such military actions of our history, our nation's deployment to Beirut is little remembered these days. In reality, there is little to remember, except that our nation called on its young defenders to go there. They did, and there, too, they died.

We commemorate these fellow Americans on Veteran's Day. Although today I am reaching three score years on this earth, Kevin was not granted that time. He will be forever in my mind's eye in the prime of life. I remember in particular his smile and laughter. It is as hearty today as it was then. We will always be together on exercises, at restaurants, or after hours, filled with good cheer, good jokes, and camaraderie.

If I were asked how best to remember those lost in skirmishes, bombings, firefights, or battles gone by, I'd say this. No one swore 'to uphold
and defend the constitution of the United States' with the intention to
die in its defense. All hoped to live, raise, or be with their families, in
a peaceful, happy world. During their military service, death came to
some. Others were wounded, and remain blind, or legless, armless, or
otherwise maimed in hospitals to this day. Some came home in body,
but their minds, some might say their souls, were damaged. We who
live owe those who suffered to stand with them in solidarity. We also
owe a debt to their families.

I think Veteran's Day should not only be celebrated by parades on the
street, but by visits to the hospital. Or perhaps we should make a phone
call, or visit one of the thousands of survivors of those who gave the
ultimate sacrifice. When we remember the dead, we should remember
the brothers, sisters, children, wives, husbands, and parents left behind
as well. The empty space of the lost parent can never be filled by words,
only by deeds, if only by a visit. There are fathers today who cry at the
very remembrance of their son's death, even decades ago. The woman
whose husband was evaporated by a direct hit should never be left to
fend for herself, particularly on Veteran's Day. The old sailor whose legs
were lost to gangrene should have visitors at his old folks' home. I recall
an old soldier I visited once at the "Altenheim" in St. Louis. I asked him
why he kept the picture of his Army Company from World War 1 on
the wall of his spare room. "So I'll never forget the boys we left beneath
the sod in France, Johnny."

Lest we forget, I'd mention one more remembrance. A battle cruiser
sailor, now 90 years old, told me this story. He said that his ship was
ordered to Murmansk, in the Soviet Union, in the early 1940's. His ship
was to recover those American sailors whose ships had been sunk by
German submarines. "One of the sailors told me his merchant ship
took a torpedo, and all hands got on board a life boat. While they float-
ed amid the wreckage, oil, and flames of their vessel, the German submarine surfaced. The Captain of the sub hailed them, and having no
choice, they rowed over to the Germans. The submariner said, 'War is

hell. I regret that I have no room for you on my ship, but here is food for you, and a map to Murmansk. Farewell.' With that, the food was delivered, and the submarine departed. The merchantmen were saved by their enemy." The old sailor's enigmatic story remained with me. I've thought much about the meaning of war as a result. Perhaps such conversations and reflections on Veteran's Day would lend it a meaning which is valuable indeed.

RAINY STREETS

Film noir came closest, with rainy streets, veiled lights, and hurried, barely observed shadows.

It suggested a door better left closed.

Yet the secret world beckoned, with its Lorelei song of intrigue, and faultless sin.

For anything was good, if there were no rules; and there were no rules, if no one knew.

Were we silent paladins of a secret war, or maybe just magicians and tricksters?

Artisans whose wounded souls needed to believe.

Beneath the gauze of cleverness or chicanery, of the hustler and distraction, were blind seekers of truth, self-liberated from the fences of the Garden.

But the door they opened was fashioned from wood of the Tree of the Knowledge of Good and Evil.

BOCCA DI VERITÀ

S ome ancient turned a Roman drain cover on its side, and affixed it to a wall.

The drain, now a mouth, became a place of 'denunciation'.

Denunciations, notes which might expose, betray, imply, incite, or cause to watch, were the essence of secrecy; of stories only partly known.

Whoever dropped the note through the 'mouth of truth' dropped a confidence.

But for whom?

HUNTING TERRORISTS

S hortly after police alerted the nation that a vehicle license plate was being sought in connection with the D.C. sniper, a citizen reported it, and an arrest was made. The alleged killer was off the street.

Recently, a waitress at a Shoney's Restaurant in Georgia notified authorities of an apparent criminal discussion she overheard. Three men seemed to be planning to bomb a building in Miami. After police investigated, the bomb plot was alleged to be a hoax. In both cases, these citizens did what any civic-minded American should do. They reported a threat to the proper authorities. Such acts are our civic duty.

Not long ago my dad and I were comparing the surprise attack on Pearl Harbor with the suicide assaults on the World Trade Center and the Pentagon.

"Something a lot of people don't remember about those days," he reflected, "is that Americans were afraid. There were rumors across the land that Japanese had landed in San Francisco, at Los Angeles, and that saboteurs and spies were everywhere. Rumors spread fear, and fear fanned more fear."

The greatest human emotion is fear, and the greatest fear is fear of the unknown. It was for that very reason that President Roosevelt reminded everyone that, "The only thing we have to fear is....fear itself."

"You can't imagine what a calming effect the president's reassurance had for everyone," dad said. "We were sucker punched at Pearl, but pulled together for the fight to come. We believed the situation was dangerous, but that the right people were doing their best to take care of the nation. And it wouldn't be over till we finished it."

Today we too might believe the enemy appears to be everywhere. He seems capable of any number of horrific means of visiting destruction on us. We feel helpless to defend ourselves against an adversary we can neither see, nor identify, nor anticipate. We feel an unspecified dread. We don't feel safe anymore. That is just what the enemy wants us to feel.

My favorite quotation came the day after the Sept. 11 attack. A German investigator, asked to comment on the apprehension of several al Qaida terrorists in Hamburg, offered this matter-of-fact observation, "Don't forget. These people are criminals. Each of these terrorists has a face, a name, and an address."

That comment, echoing President Bush's determined assurance that we will patiently but relentlessly pursue these killers anywhere they may hide, did much to reassure Americans.

But how, Americans ask, can we take part? We want to pull together, so what do we do? The answer has been here all along; we've known it intuitively, but never until now really had an immediate need in this generation to act upon it. We know that loose lips sink ships. But now we know that our eyes catch spies...and the criminal killers they report to.

Each of the terrorists has a face, a name, and an address, and now they too know fear. Their leaders have abandoned them, world law enforcement is seeking them, and every day more Americans become more astute in what to watch for and report.

There are many practical hurdles to overcome, and the road won't be easy.

Whereas yesterday we weren't aware, today we know who to call if something just doesn't seem right. We help each other. Americans are pulling together. We watch our surroundings in ways we didn't before.

We are protecting ourselves, informing ourselves, and not letting fear defeat us before we've entered the fight. No one today will turn away if a security problem seems to require a solution. We offer assistance to others and make sure someone takes action to protect us. If we see a better way, we speak up.

The only thing we have to fear is fear itself. Remember that every terrorist has a face, a name, and an address. We'll get them if we help each other. We are a quarter billion Americans whose eyes are watching in restaurants, at gas stations, in the office, and on the road.

Now the cowards who murdered our people really have something to fear.

We are out to get them.

FOUR FREEDOMS REVISITED

Presented at the "Us versus Them" conference, Szczecin, Poland.

In the darkest days of the Great Depression, President Franklin Delano Roosevelt stood on the steps of the American Capitol and spoke these words, "So, first of all, let me assert my firm belief that the only thing we have to fear is fear itself -- nameless, unreasoning, unjustified terror which paralyzes needed efforts to convert retreat into advance."

More powerful, memorable, and truer words were seldom spoken. They came at a time when an unreasoning fear of the future was common across the entire world. Many feared that there would be no end to a world of woe beset by massive unemployment and the seemingly unstoppable rise of Nazi, Soviet, and Japanese dictatorships.

Some 68 years later dread fear fell again across the world. On a calm, September day in 2001 unspeakable horror struck viciously, violently, ruthlessly. A sneak attack originating from seemingly nowhere took place: aircraft carrying innocent civilians were hijacked and piloted by desperate murderers into the World Trade Center in New York City. The aftermath of that day left a world dumbstruck by bewilderment, confusion, and the trembling silence of aimless fear.

I speak as a linguist, an investigator, a teacher, and a retired soldier. We've learned much since those days. We've learned the assault was the act of a small group of driven, delusional fanatics, **not** the Muslim world. This is not a clash of cultures; it is rather the mundane pursuit of a large criminal enterprise. The lead murderer was a wealthy man whose business imagination enlisted desperate people. His business was as an entrepreneurial Murder Incorporated. He proposed unleashing worldwide, heartless, merciless revenge for a litany of evils that he proclaimed had been visited upon the Islamic world by the West, the Jews, and Muslim traitors.

The reality is that he only exploited fear. He was, like Adolf Hitler before him, a balladeer of lies, a conductor of the orchestra of revenge, murder, and chaos. He grasped deep into the reservoir of resentment, fear, and loss that characterized the Muslim world, and played it to his own advantage. Nowhere, however, has his enterprise raised a society of hope, only a culture of death. His view was massively, overwhelmingly rejected in the Muslim world.

My theme is that ten years ago, on that September day, a criminal enterprise struck a deep and abiding wound. It was a criminal enterprise characterized by a cadre of Western-educated but disillusioned, directionless, and unassimilated young Muslims, not the Muslim world. This extremist cadre of ideologues in turn exploited largely uneducated Muslim foot soldiers around the world. These latter were truly oppressed, and their oppression was itself exploited by that corporate, clandestine leadership.

Today let me offer my hope, how "we" can learn to live in a world with "them." I propose that we should deal with the terrorist leadership not through relentless warfare, but rather through international law enforcement and Special Forces cooperation. We should deal with this dedicated cadre of bitter fanatics just as we dealt with European terrorism in the 1980's. For the followers of this fanatical cadre, however, we can employ diplomacy, dialogue, education, reconciliation, and foreign exchange projects to break down the wall of fear among average Muslims. Lastly, we ourselves must learn more about the larger, dispossessed world that was so ruthlessly brought to our attention; we are a part of that world.

I would like to offer this hope simply, with a straightforward appeal to first principles from our American history. These principles, if acted upon by all people of good will, can bring terrorists and the fever swamps in which they thrive, to their knees. I speak here of the

Four Freedoms introduced by our own President Roosevelt in the dark spring of 1941.

FIRST, HE INTRODUCED AS A GOAL FOR ALL PEACEABLE PEOPLE, THE FREEDOM OF SPEECH.

I am addressing some who in living memory experienced the terrors brought about by another fantasist, Adolf Hitler. It was Hitler who exploited the fears of a nation that had been defeated in the First World War, and so he deluded the German people, a people then virtually starving in the midst of the worldwide Depression. His web of lies and half-truths, and his manipulation of fear, distrust, betrayal and revenge mythologies, led to war.

No sooner had the war ended than a further catastrophe was visited on the long-suffering people of Eastern Europe: forty years of Communist dictatorship. Throughout this entire time no-one but the government was allowed to speak. Only presentations that had been cleared by government bureaucrats were published, or heard.

Today, we need to see speech not only as what we do, but what we can hear or read as well. We must encourage a culture that learns multiple languages. Language opens the door to what the 'other' thinks, in ways a translation does not. We must encourage a nation of travelers. We must not only be world travelers, but virtual travelers on a free and independent Internet. We must encourage national programs that exchange students for long periods with other lands, the better to introduce students in one nation to another. By exposing our fellow citizens and students to other cultures through projects such as the American Peace Corps, the Turkish Gulen Movement, the Goethe House programs, Farmer to Farmer, and a host of others, we make our world more understandable, and so less fearful. As another American President, Abraham Lincoln, said, "Do I not destroy my enemy when I make him my friend?"

Next, Roosevelt proposed the Freedom of Worship.

Returning from war-torn Sarajevo a friend of mine once showed me a picture. It was a panorama of the city taken from a distant hillside. I remarked that it showed all sorts of snow on the mountains surrounding the city.

"Didn't you just return from a short trip in July?" I asked him.

"Where'd all this snow come from?"

"That's not snow," he quietly commented, "those are tombstones on graves".

In a world beset by religious intolerance and Bosnian-style ethnic cleansing, where the word Srebrenica carries a death knell when spoken, I propose the right to freedom of worship as an antidote. If I can build my church, my synagogue, my mosque, or my school in your country, and we see interfaith social outreach as something we can do together, we've chipped away another brick in the wall of intolerance. In my city of Huntsville, Alabama, an Interfaith Mission Service was created forty years ago to disarm mistrust before it started. Young people of the Christian, Muslim, Jewish and other faiths work together on community projects. This is just as they do in the center for reconciliation near Auschwitz, or Oswiecim, Poland, today.

Three-and-a-half centuries ago, my family fled from England to escape religious persecution. The first law ever enacted on the North American continent conferring religious liberty was written by those settlers in what was then the Crown colony of Maryland. No law exists today which blocks my, or anyone else's, public practice of faith in America. Any nation that seeks to join our future should look to that as a right.

Freedom from Want.

My father-in-law fought the Nazis in World War II. Once we were discussing where Hitler's foot soldiers came from, and he offered a very simple observation he had heard from a German he met after the war. "If you are the father of a family, by the time the seventh meal you can't provide for your children comes around, you are ready to follow anyone who will give it to you." If we want to avoid giving terrorists water for the garden of resentment, revenge, and hatred, we have to ensure a world of solidarity. That means, I must be able to provide for my family, or it will be quite easy for me to fall under the spell of a mesmerizing liar, a clever deceiver, or a terrorist. Take this truism to any level: to nation, to religion, to the entire world. As educators, we must ensure we can instill in our students the belief that it really is a world of one for all, and all for one. In any society, when the bottom line of financial profit takes primacy of place over care for the least able, least accepted, most defenseless among us, we are truly doomed. We will surely have a fight on our hands. A society is characterized by how it takes care of those least able to care for themselves. So, today, in our world, no terrorist can exploit anyone who knows and understands that his neighbor, be he just down the block, or all the way across the world, is someone with dignity just like his own.

My sister could never walk. My family, my father's union, even our government helped make her life in some ways better. You can't hate what you know is an enterprise that ultimately cares about you. As long as we can try to ensure this is true in our own countries, in our own ways, then the appeal of the bomber can only be diminished.

FREEDOM FROM FEAR.

My favorite quotation from the days after 9/11 came from the Director of German police, who had been investigating a terrorist cell in Hamburg, Germany. He said in a very businesslike and matter of fact manner, "Let's remember, these terrorists are criminals. They all have a name, a face, and an address. We'll get them." Such confidence, such patient, thoughtful, relentless pursuit of criminals is what we need. We fight terrorists, not evil incarnate. But the battle of international law against the terrorist is more than this.

I speak as a soldier and civil servant who has long been involved in the secret battle against terrorists, from the days of the Red Army Faction, the Red Brigades, and others, to this very day. The fight against the murderer, the terrorist, is a fight against his goal to inflict a nameless terror, which makes us tremble with a directionless fear. That's what their beheadings, their bombings, their video interrogations, their suicide killings seek to inflict on us. They win when we change because of their crimes.

In 1984, a Catholic priest, Jerzy Popilusko, was murdered by the Communist secret police. He was slain because he had demanded the right to speak and worship freely, and for his nation not to live in want or fear. He said, "Overcoming fear is a key element in the process of setting Man free. Fear springs from threat. We fear suffering; we fear the loss of some goods, the loss of freedom, health or job. This fear makes us act against our conscience and it is by means of conscience that we measure Truth. We overcome fear the moment we agree to lose something for the sake of higher values. If Truth becomes a value worth suffering for, worth taking a risk, then we will overcome fear that keeps us in slavery."

Terrorist violence can only continue to exist so long as a person does not see the "other" as a being with dignity, no matter who he might be, or what he might believe. The fear terrorists hope to spread can be overcome, and the terrorists brought to justice. They only win when their terror becomes our reality. It is fear that causes us to attack blindly, to live in fear of those we don't understand, and thus provide an even greater chance for terrorism to take root. Change should only come about for the common good, by the common agreement of people of good will, not because someone fears a bomber.

Remember, Solidarity forever, and the truth will make us free.

CLASS IS OVER

Mysterious meetings in distant lands were only part of his repertoire. It's like he told you a story which lacked nothing but an ending. He spoke in riddles, but we were enabled to learn dark techniques nonetheless. What if he weren't here, how would I know what to do, who to talk to? I remember how much I believed. I wanted so much to trust him. He seemed the best, someone I wanted to be like; no, he was the best. Then he left, and I was left.

KRAKOW'S MEMORIALS

Two landmarks are visible on the air approach to the UNES-CO protected ancient city of Krakow, Poland. The first is a scar on the landscape which marks a disused stone quarry. Its gray walls now arc round a lake. The second is the vast, gray, metal pipe and concrete ganglia of the mammoth Nova Huta steelworks with its surrounding blocks of flats which house a quarter million people. These Stalin era buildings look like gravestones lined up row by row. Both places played a role in my life, and I was on a sort of pilgrimage there.

After a couple wonderful days spent exploring the medieval streets, castle, and cathedral of Krakow, my wife and I went to visit the now international Jagellonian University. In the University Church we met a young Irishman man who by chance had come there. He told us he always went to a church when he was lost. He'd been given wrong directions and so was wandering until he went into the church where we met.

We were able to help him as he, like us, was on a quest to understand a little more about Pope John Paul II, who studied in and was once Bishop of Krakow. I mentioned the rock quarry we'd seen where, as young Karol Wojtyla, the future Pope John Paul worked during the Second World War. Yes, our Irish acquaintance knew that place, for he was a gravedigger, "about as close as you come to a quarryman these days." He commented that John Paul II understood workers like him, because blasting and chiseling rock is hard, manual labor. "And he studied for the priesthood secretly at night. I'm afraid I just go home and fall asleep."

We explained how to get to Nova Huta, just outside of Krakow, where one of John Paul's most defining moments occurred. It was there, when as Bishop, he showed how to defeat an all powerful enemy using peaceful methods and prayer.

It has been said that all too often the good people of the world win righteous moral victories, or noble self awareness, while the evil win the real estate. Nova Huta was for years such a place. Built by Stalin's orders in 1948 as a foil to the Catholic, ancient Polish capital of Krakow, Nova Huta was to be a city without God. After a decade of social strife, permission to build a church was finally granted in 1966. A huge cross was placed on a green space, and outdoor services were held there. More years of bureaucratic aggravation, switched sites, and cynical lies by the Communist government held up any construction. Of course, no permission would ever have been granted had it not been for the newly assigned Catholic Bishop, Karol Wojtyla. He was shocked by the street fighting that took place when the Communists came to take down even the cross which stood for so long at the open field. So he organized religious processions through the streets. He held mass prayers in the fields, in all sorts of weather; in the snow and in the rain. Relentlessly, but prayerfully, the contest continued. They never gave up. Then one day the government gave in.

Of course, there were caveats. To build the church, it was stipulated no state earthmovers, no concrete mixers, nor construction material could be used. And it all belonged to the Communist state in those days. Not a 'gram of Lenin works steel' could be used or sold to those who wanted that church. It was never, ever intended by the government to allow the church to be built.

So the Bishop asked every future parishioner to bring stones. Hundreds, then thousands, then literally millions of stones were brought in bags, in pockets, in suitcases. The cement was mixed with shovels in wooden boxes made for the purpose. Just like the ancient cathedrals of old, the church grew stone by stone, made literally by hand by those for whom it meant so much, for which some of them had died.

Bishop Wojtyla was present at the Second Vatican Council in the early 1960's, having been given last minute permission to depart for it by the

Polish Communist government. As he prepared to return to Krakow, he was approached by Pope Paul VI, who handed him a stone. Let this stone be the foundation of the Church you are building in Nova Huta, he offered. And so it was. That stone was taken from the ground of St. Peter's tomb in Rome. It was laid in place by Bishop Wojtyla in Nova Huta. That stone has seen raised over it the multi-million stone church which is shaped like...a ship. And over the stone sides of the church is a brown slate 'deck', over which a towering 'mast' commemorates the much defended cross which began the long, long construction process.

As a young father I saw a picture in a magazine of the completed church in 1977. Although it was located in a land beyond the Iron Curtain, it had a peaceful aspect which I can still see in my mind's eye today. It looked like a sort of ship floating over the sea of gray apartment blocks. It was dedicated to Christ's mother, but the locals call it even today the Lord's Ark. I wanted one day to visit that place, because it meant so much to so many, even in its painful Calvary of construction. I wanted to be a part of that someday.

Almost thirty years later I did. The Lord's Ark's bells were donated by the Dutch; the artwork inside is captivating. It tells the viewer about the people who worship there. Christ's way of the Cross is commemorated in a huge mural which tells the story of Christ's last hours through vignettes of the sufferings of the people of Poland. Here is a Pole in prisoner's rags, beaten by a Nazi. There is a statue of St. Maximilian Kolbe, a priest who volunteered to be murdered in place of another man at Auschwitz, just as Christ did for us. Again there is a statue of the Blessed Mother made from shrapnel and bullets taken from the flesh of Polish soldiers wounded in the World War, and here a holy mother whose sons were taken to Siberia. Just as they suffered, so did Christ before them and for them.

The altar is a sort of marble hand, from which the bread of life is taken; the tabernacle, where the sacred hosts are kept, recalls with otherworldly metals the mighty God who made the universe with its planets and stars. Indeed, embedded in that sacred space is a moon rock, given

by the people of the United States. Then there is the astounding, crucified Christ, who though fashioned in a sort of tortured cruciform is not
affixed to a cross. Christ knew real pain as did the Poles; but he is risen,
as are they from oppression.

So we gave our Irish acquaintance directions to the Lord's Ark in Nova
Huta, and together we laughed because now he would need only look
for the ship on the gray waves. And so he went, with our good wishes.
The place he would find is where once a bishop laid the cornerstone for
a church, and himself later became the rock of the Church itself.

I'll always remember Michael, our Irishman, because he unwittingly
summarized what meant so much to me about that pilgrimage. Over
the 'reconciliation chapel' which a visitor enters first in that uniquely
designed Church of Our Lady of Poland, the Lord's Ark, there is an in-
scription which says, "Before entering, reconcile with God, with your
neighbors, and with yourself." Whenever I'm lost, I'll go to a church.

MARCH OF THE LIVING

Thousands of international marchers including students, technicians, teachers, rabbis, and even a Catholic Bishop, wound along a two mile route from Auschwitz Concentration Camp to the dreaded Auschwitz-Birkenau, scene of industrialized slaughter. This was not a dread trudge of despair, but rather a vital presence. It was a sign to the entire world that hope and the zeal for justice through remembrance had triumphed. The 22,000 participants in the March of the Living 2005 were in Poland to show solidarity with those who fight daily against intolerance in all its morbid variations, by recalling what happened when hate prevails.

As we wound through a tiny settlement enroute, the mammoth former camp administration building emerged into view. Its central tower, obscured by a misty rain against grey skies, brooded over the arcade under which the death trains once passed. Slowly, the camp's perimeter came into view. The inmates' barracks were ranked behind guard towers that went on, and on, and even further on. The panorama of what once was the secret murder center of the Thousand Year Reich astounded this first time viewer by its relentlessness.

As we neared the camp, hundreds of wooden signs, each no larger than a small book, were posted haphazardly in that railroad spur which drew millions to their doom. "We'll never forget", "We were here mother", "Never again", and thousands of names--and even pictures-- of loved ones all some sixty years dead, were scattered along the track. Poignantly, most often seen was the simple invocation "Remember", in dozens of languages.

Inside, the efficiency of the plan to kill Europe's Jews manifested itself. In a barbed wire enclosure an entire train of animal cars could be emptied of people, some of whom were dead in their own waste from suffocation, starvation, heat and thirst. The survivors were divided into those who could work, and those who could not. The latter would be marched off to long, low buildings, shaved of all body hair, stripped naked, marched into concrete gas chambers, murdered and cremated in under an hour and a half. One hour and a half.

Often, truth is borne in simple signs. The kingdom of deceit that was the Nazi empire was revealed clearly to me by the stolen high heeled shoes, kept with thousands of others for shipment back to Germany. High heeled shoes seemed a sort of metaphor; that the largely Jewish victims convinced themselves that surely the 'resettlement' from their homes to the "East" could not end in death. But it did. It did because the world did not know, did not want to know or knowing, did nothing about it. Even the United States Government, shown indisputable proof of the slaughter going on in that place, would not divert bombers to blow up the tracks and so slow down the massacre machine. The endless Nazi euphemisms; that they were simply resettling the Jews, or creating Jewish cities as in Theresienstadt, or that the there was a "Rose Garden" in Majdanek (which really referred to blood sprinkled on the ground there), or that the Erntefest, or Autumn Festival was something other than a brutal massacre of thousands of Jewish prisoners killed in cold blood, allowed the world to deny reality by believing lies. How the Nazi bully boys must have laughed at those whose decadence preferred self deceit to searching out the truth and doing something. And all while the trains rolled ever onward. A crime so titanic astounds even as it shames, as we try to understand.

Where does all this leave us, who see or read about this today? Are we not our brother's keeper? Is not the simplest injunction, to do unto others as we would have them do unto us, something that unites us today? Where are we in all this, we who today inhabit this world, at this time in this place, which less than two generations ago offered up the least among us to Moloch?

Mother Theresa of Calcutta said we must try to do good, even if we fail in the attempt. Try, no matter what the cost, added Pope John Paul

II. We are not called to be successful, only faithful. A traveler with us, who survived the extermination camp at Majdanek, said his daily prayer during his time in that horrific place was a Psalm of lamentation which began "From out of the depths I cry to you O Lord. Make haste to help me." He did not need to speak the prayer, a cry for help from a son to a beloved Father, because he lived it every day. He lived to tell us, in anecdotal asides during our wanderings through those places, that his faith saved him, even as his rational mind at the time caused him to ask where God was, or indeed whether God existed.

Today the Nazi regime is gone; their racial theories considered antique, even bizarre if not laughable conceits of the past. In their secret torture and gas chambers free men and women gather today and discuss what it all meant; that such evil could prevail for the time that it did. Perhaps one thought stays with me, carved in stone over the ossuary of thousands murdered at Majdanek, "Let our loss be your warning."

The lie over Auschwitz's main gate reads *Arbeit Macht Frei* (work makes you free). The legacy of Nazism is the lie, the lash and prisons. The best homage we can pay to truth, as James Russell Lowell remarked, is to use it.

Be warned; be aware how fragile our precious liberties are when men seek to demean, persecute, and hurt others. Respect and tolerance, for even the least among us, protects us all. We each reflect a divine spark. Do unto others, as you would have them do unto you, every day. We are all in this together.

NEUTRALS

Eight flat, gray tombstones stand out in the tiny cemetery, because they are all alike.

They are lined up next to one another among memorials for long dead subjects of an Empire, citizens of an unfortunate Republic, and modern times.

These eight were memorable, if only because joined in death. All died one night during an Allied bombing run in July, 1944.

Sure, long stories can seek to explain what brought it about, or why it was necessary.

But the dead 84 year old mother, whose family name just by chance was the same as an old friend in America, struck me.

Along with the others, a child, and some younger boys and women, all were killed by phosphorus and high explosive bombs.

I keep forgetting the point of why all this was necessary; but it made me doubt the belief that science is morally neutral.

RELIGIOUS FREEDOM

My first relative to emigrate to America came to the colony of Maryland. He came as a refugee from religious persecution. The England he left made it unlawful for him to practice his faith openly; taxed him if he did, forbade him to hold office, and took his property and inheritance. The death penalty was still in effect. To its eternal historical credit, Maryland instituted the first act of religious toleration in British America. Residents could practice their faith, without fear of persecution. This was in the mid-17th century, some 360 years ago.

Now, these many years on, we are a nation of many, many faiths. Our Constitution guarantees *Congress shall make no law respecting an establishment of religion, or prohibiting the free exercise thereof.* Often, we Americans believe the world concurs with this. This is not true. We are part of a world where governments persecute religion, and where social controls limit it. Often, violation of either of these controls results in death for those who believe differently.

Our leaders are often confronted with dilemmas that seem to offer no way out. Some of our closest allies disallow the free practice of other religions, just as England did those hundreds of years ago. I recall during Operation Desert Storm American troops had to be quietly exempted from Saudi Arabian law that forbade the practice of any religion other than the Muslim faith, as it is practiced in that kingdom. Today, China under its Communist government represses the practice of the Christian faith to any who do not adhere to strictly regulated 'national religious' organizations. Recently, they even took away an orphanage because the local bishop refused to join the so-called Patriotic church. In some countries, one can be executed for converting others, or converting himself, to another faith. Indeed, the world is a complex place.

What to do? It is too facile to say religion is a private matter. Tyrannies use this standard ploy. They want no activity to oppose them, so restrict any 'practice' of religion to a place where it can be monitored and controlled. This sham 'acceptance' of religion rewards submission, where for instance religious leaders are rewarded who toe the government line. 30 pieces of silver are even today being offered for betrayal of one's faith. I remember well when we once visited St. Hedwig's Cathedral in then Communist East Berlin. The parishioners of the church were kneeling in prayer, while hovering in back of the pews were two black-trench coated secret policemen. They were clearly writing down information on those present. The tense atmosphere was beyond description. To think back on that time causes me to shudder at the reality of that event. I could leave when I wanted, but those who lived there risked their very freedom while Gestapo-like thugs hovered over their moments of prayer. Religious liberty, Communist style. Today, the thugs have different names, but the threats are the same, or worse.

Today, religious zealots blow up those who disagree with them in mosques in Iraq, Christian churches in Egypt, and a host of other places of worship. All suffer at the hands of killers and persecutors who worship a false god of death.

Common sense knows a man's conscience informs his most personal choices. For this reason religion, understood as that which binds a person's worldview together, can never be wholly separated from a role in a person's political actions. Religion must inform principles, and principles inform the citizen. Better said, religion should always be free to inform the public discussion, and so the conscience of the listener. Religion must not become a political party. Religion, properly understood, with liberty to preach, proselytize, and worship freely, can only ennoble a society. No law need promote a religion, but no nation should act against any faith, peacefully expressed. Just as no law should hinder its practice, no one should suffer social ostracism or worse for practicing or sharing his faith openly and peacefully. No one need fear a church in Saudi Arabia any more than a mosque in New York, if the believers in them seek dialogue, reconciliation, and peace.

Over 100 years ago, at the opening of the Great Louisiana Purchase Exposition, the St. Louis World's Fair of 1904, Cardinal John Glennon gave this invocation before the assembled crowd and its keynote speaker, President Teddy Roosevelt.

"We pray Thee, O God of might, wisdom, and justice, through whom authority is rightly administered, laws are enacted, and judgment decreed, assist with thy holy spirit of counsel and fortitude, the President of these United States. That his administration may be conducted in right counsel, and may be committed in righteousness, and be eminently useful to thy people over whom he presides; by encouraging a respect for virtue and religion, by faithful execution of the laws in justice and mercy, and by restraining vice and immorality.

Let the light of thy divine wisdom direct the deliberations of Congress and shine forth in all their proceedings and laws framed for our rule and government so that they may tend to the preservation of peace, the promotion of national happiness, the increase of industry, sobriety, and useful knowledge, and may perpetuate to us the blessings of equal liberty.

After his speech, President Roosevelt concluded, "I hope I may be permitted to suggest that our thoughts and surroundings on this occasion should lead us to humble recognition of the providence of God in all that has made us a great nation." Both speakers struck the perfect balance of church and state.

OPAQUE

German forests, green woven in gray, cloud the perception.

Heavy, muted Tannenbaum, angled hardwoods, stress and crack.

With a vest, ascot, sensible imported British country clothes; he was a good 'Bürgerlich' citizen.

Every Sunday, he walked his Weimaraner through miles of trails surrounding the village.

Counter surveillance. He never saw us.

He'd never see us. We weren't there.

We found him because someone, perhaps in Berlin, perhaps at a conference,

Betrayed him for money, for spite, but most likely knew him only as a name somewhere.

It almost always ends this way.

TABLE TALK

S omehow, a Gasthaus was a place to learn the truth.

Crisp tablecloths, wholesome log walls; here a doctor felt at ease to reveal a secret.

Most valuable, my friend confided, "No one comes to the secret world unless something is broken, or missing, in his life."

Another time, in a place I only remember because of its incongruous blue Star of David high in a far window,

A simple laborer confessed he was working for the "East Bloc".

Drunk, he couldn't go on anymore. He'd expended his courage.

I learned later the Star might have come from the synagogue which once stood across the street.

Another secret.

RECRUITMENT

S ecrecy itself was the appeal. All the secrecy in my life would be made right. All secrecy's handmaidens; hidden motives, duplicity, betrayal, and lies, were no longer measures of shame, but rather virtuous, even patriotic.

How did they know they had found just the right person? How could they have known, for I had found them, didn't I? Their joy was truly mine, and I'd found my muse. We loved each other, for love is without guile. Until it is time to love another.

THE SMALLEST BETRAYAL

He came to us from the sea, a sailor who swam ashore in Libya. And we believed the baptism cleansed him.

He confirmed our every hope when it seemed he married a fellow Russian expatriate, lonely, in far away England.

Secure, settled, he spoke in tongues what we wanted to believe. For decades, Radio Free Europe never had anyone such as he.

His paramour, and a four year old, came into our lives long after his wife left.

His little girl was as our own child when we watched her for them; the sparkle of things hoped for.

Yet his baptism was that of a shape shifter, his confirmation a side show sham.

Disembodied, he reappeared in Moscow, a carnival magician who walked through the Wall.

He denounced us, renounced us all as frauds, fronts for the imperialist intelligence services.

His friend shed the tears of an actress, until she too was arrested as a spy.

Only the smallest betrayal remained, and she was taken away, too.

WHAT THE NEW AMERICAN FOUND

Seldom in this age of governmental intransigence and 'no compromise' does a real event bolt us back to recognition of what truly defines America. I realized this on a recent business flight. As green Texas fields dissolved into brown crags and canyons, my aisle mate's story became even more arresting. I lost all sense of the aircraft engines outside as this stranger told me of her grandfather. During the Second World War, this average man of Budapest, Hungary, secretly risked his life by hiding resistance fighters on the run and Jews pursued for racial murder. Through a well wrought redesign of his warehouse, repeated Nazi searches turned up not a single wanted person. This daily fear lasted years. When the war was over, all hoped for an end to Gestapo-style police state terror. It was not to be, for Stalin's Red Army ensured a brutish Red terror came next.

Living quietly throughout the worst of Stalin's Communist control of that country, he tried to stay away from politics. Because he had aided the underground against the Nazis during the war, he was not treated to one or another of the Communist dungeons reserved for so-called counter-revolutionaries. With the great Hungarian revolt against Communism in 1956, the now quite elderly grandfather decided to join the freedom movement. They lost when Soviet tanks rolled into Budapest, and those not murdered outright, executed, or exiled to Siberia were thrown into prison. Among the latter was her grandfather.

I learned of my traveling companion's life since the fall of Communism. She and her husband, both highly educated engineers, lived in various lands throughout the world. Yet here they were in America, some 11 years now. Their children were at ease with their American friends, and were for all the world American. We discussed languages, and shared what made language study of such value. Through language we learn not only how another people speaks, but the meaning behind such words they might use. She noted that whenever, for example, an American uses the word freedom, or liberty, it means something special. It is quite different from a European or an Asian. "How do you mean? I asked. "Take for instance freedom to do what you want. In some countries, you will never leave the group you are born into. Here, you can do anything you want to try. Americans have life, liberty, and the pursuit of happiness. No other country makes happiness a part of their goal."

I had long forgotten the book I brought along, and she held a pamphlet open on her lap. She said she was going to study this as we flew, but it was interesting talking about these things. "You see," she said, "This is my study guide for the citizenship test! In three weeks I have my citizenship test." For the rest of the trip we discussed the meaning of the 4th of July for Americans, the Constitution, and even the Bill of Rights. Most interesting were her civics questions, which dealt with how our government works. We discussed checks and balances, and how each separate part of government had powers to limit those of the other parts. Even as we discussed present day events, where each segment of government argued its case, one aspect of American government was clear. Compromise made the system work. I recalled a quotation from an 18th Century British statesman I had heard in a hot St. Louis classroom decades ago. The British Parliamentarian Edmund Burke, who argued for English reconciliation with America, said, "All government, indeed every human benefit and enjoyment, every virtue and every prudent act, is founded on compromise and barter."

Great men of that distant age saw to it that government by the one, the few, and the many; by the President, Supreme Court, and Congress, would be subject to human contention. Each had to balance the power of the other. The only way to do this was compromise. "And that makes for the pursuit of happiness," my new found American friend said.

FRAGMENT

".....eternally a stranger who condemns himself---never to know real peace...."
Fragment of a poem written by the Soviet spy, Richard Sorge, executed by the Japanese in 1944, found among his personal effects.

This is all we have of you.

After all, what we thought we knew of you was only your personality displayed for Japanese colleagues and German friends,

Who knew you as the publicly confident, affable, and eminently connected bon vivant,

Where did you go for peace of soul?

Where neither wit, nor cleverness can hide; how did you deal with the duplicity, which this enigmatic phrase betrays?

Is this your poem the reality of any espionage? This self judgment is even harsher than death.

Is this an autobiography?

FAIRPLAY

Drenched, he was friendly enough.

An English investigator whose life in the secret world weighed heavily upon him.

His dripping overcoat on the chair, the coffee seemed particularly good now that the rain was pounding outside the window.

He'd laughed with me as we shared those tales which tell who we are, or want others to know.

Yet his was particularly revealing.

"Chasing gunmen up and down County Antrim was grueling. Whenever we'd appear, they'd be long away.

I guess I thought my job done to give chase, and theirs to skip ahead.

Until I heard not one of them could vote unless he owned property. And this in the land of the Mother of Parliaments! What would I do if it were me? I was never so sure of certainties after that.

Perhaps I could see another man clearer, in light of such things. Perhaps, fairplay and all that."

A FOUNDING MOTHER

Who could believe the Israeli adventure the old grandmother in Germany experienced? And why did she tell me? I learned more about the toughness of Israel, and the endurance and resilience of her people from this lady than from any lecture or speech I ever heard. In so doing, I learned a valuable truth about the Middle East. But that jumps ahead in my story.

On a warm, moist night in the Frankenland foothills of Bavaria, I took a walk after a day of conferences. As I returned to my hotel, two older ladies asked the way downtown. Their German sounded very antique and formal, very pre-war. They were Israelis. They were Jews, and both grandmothers. I commented that it was unusual, was it not, for Israelis to vacation here in Germany? They smiled and said that it was a homecoming, of sorts. They were born in the old Europe, the Europe before the war. They were born during the old Weimar Republic days. One was a resident at that time of the free port city of Danzig. Her father was a city councilman. She paused, and wondered how she had told so much, that surely I wasn't interested. I asked her to please continue. She told this tale.

"One day, in 1939, my father came home from work. He was deeply troubled. He had just come from a secret Zionist meeting. 'The Germans will invade,' he said, 'There will be war.' Of course, those of us young people in the family paid little attention. Although I was sixteen, I cared little about politics. My world blossomed before me. I was a young and happy girl. "

"Father said we must prepare to leave. Then Mother began to cry. So did the little ones, because Mother was. She did not want to leave her home of generations. Nor did Father, but he feared the worst. He knew what the Germans did to the Jews in Germany, and did not want to wait for their conquest of Danzig. Uncle said it would not be bad, the Germans talked loud but did little actual harm.

"By now, all the children were crying, for no one wanted to leave friends and classmates. In time it was decided to leave, but there was only room on the ship for Mother and me. We left in an illegal ship bound from the port of Danzig to British Palestine. "My father said he would stay, and try to join us later. He would watch over our family left behind.

"Our ship sailed secretly at night through the Baltic Sea. We sailed around Denmark, France and Spain. We stayed warm as best we could, crowded below decks. Mother became sick, and I couldn't help her."

The old lady started crying, and became embarrassed. Then, with the faraway eyes that look upon long ago events, she continued.

"We approached the coast of Palestine in the pitch black of a moonless night. We dropped anchor. In the distance we heard the approach of a boat. Then a klieg-light beamed on us! The British! We were captured!

"Our ship was brought under escort to Haifa, Palestine, where we were unloaded and processed. Then we were put back on the ship and told to leave Palestine forever. We were illegal immigrants! We were to return to our "point of origin" which our captain claimed was Nicosia in Cyprus. A Haifa processing pen was all my mother ever saw of Palestine.

"Upon our sad deportation, Mother worsened. She could not get her breath and I could do nothing. We had no medicine. The next day my mother died at sea." A light mist had begun, it glistened together with the tears on her old face.

"Cyprus did not want us, so we managed to secretly lease another ship for a second desperate attempt. The grown men made secret contacts. One night, about six hundred of us, crammed in a launch, set out again for Palestine.

"Again the shore was black. One of the boys dove overboard and swam until we lost sight of him. The wait seemed forever. Then he returned, in a boat, piloted by a man who greeted us in Hebrew! We were saved!"

Then the old woman paused. She looked straight at me and with a broken voice cried, "Everyone in Danzig was taken by the Nazis. The Nazis killed them all. And my Mother, also dead! I was all alone in the world."

She began to cry uncontrollably. I held her shoulder and said, "But now your children have you, and you have them. That makes you one of the founding mothers of Israel, doesn't it?"

She looked at me, and said, "Yes, a founding mother." And then she smiled, as did I. The rest of our visit continued over tea at the hotel café, watching the now damp German street outside. Her boys were professionals, one a doctor at a kibbutz, the other a fighter pilot. She was very proud of them. She was a pioneer, a founding mother who had helped make a home and a country. People like that will never run away again. That was a valuable truth about the Middle East I learned that warm German night.

CEMETERY VISIT

Cemeteries are where I prefer to visit.

I remember you left your charming white heather flowers at Rodney Ford's grave, Clearly visible as I strolled along graveled lanes.

The surrounding trees planted by his long ago relatives were now so poignant; Willows weeping for Rodney.

And you chose white heather. A sound choice, for they symbolize protection from danger.

Or did you know that? Or was it just that no one else would choose that type flower, which meetings such as ours required?

But you'd know I'd calculate the numbers, 18 for R, six for F.

And find you a day later at the designated time, in the agreed upon room, for which Rodney pointed the way.

Odd, when you think of it. Was Rodney a patriot because of this, or only another of the exploited?

THINKING ABOUT 9/11 AFTER MANY YEARS

We will all reflect upon the horrors of 9/11. Who cannot see this monumental Shakespearean tragedy for the drama, human sorrow, and murderous evil it revealed? Perhaps a quiet reflection on a similar time, some years ago, may help us understand this in some perspective.

London burned for days. Ancient streets, known since medieval times, collapsed in flame, ash, rubble, and cinder. Threadneedle Street, entire swaths of Covent Garden, Shoe Street and hundreds more were demolished by a malevolent act of men. This aerial bombing 'Blitz' by Hitler's Luftwaffe in 1940 was designed to wreck British industry and massacre its men, women, and children. Yet amidst the horrors of death by fire, asphyxiation, collapsing stone, brick, and concrete, a common wildflower was observed to grow in exceptional abundance. As one careworn, exhausted teacher said, "A lot of flowers grew on the bombed spaces, especially one in particular. It was a stalk with a lot of little red spots. It was like a weed really. It was called 'London Pride'." It was an everyday flower, yet its resilience, indeed its very expansive survivability became a sort of metaphor for Londoners. Here was something the Germans and all their might could not touch. It grew despite fire and high explosives, incendiaries and steel shrapnel. It reappeared everywhere, through rubble, twisted iron posts, and abandoned demolished homes and warehouses.

Another Englishman, sitting in a bombed out London railroad station, was inspired by the little flower to write a song, which became a watchword of Londoners' resilience and never-say-die attitude. Noel Coward was struck, as he said, by a palpable nostalgia and sentimentality, and wrote the song "London Pride" while bombs up above destroyed the things and places he knew.

London Pride has been handed down to us,
London Pride is a flower that's free.
London Pride means our own dear town to us.
And our Pride it forever will be.

 His pride was in the London, which quite literally was being ruthlessly destroyed as he wrote. Homes, monuments, churches, stores, passages, architectural wonders and common street dwellings were going up in a Gotterdammerung caused by Nazi fury.

Yet Noel Coward knew that London was more than its streets and stores, its homes and even its living people. It was a sense of place, of belonging. London was the cumulative reality of generations of Londoners.

In our city darkened now, street and square and crescent,
We can feel our living past in our shadowed present,
Ghosts beside our starlit Thames
Who lived and loved and died
Keep throughout the ages London Pride.

Can we who have suffered our own losses learn from that long ago London experience? It seems what material wealth Londoners had was indeed ground to dust by droning, death spewing bombers. Each day London's people emerged to yet further carnage, debris, and a burning Inferno. Yet each day they emerged, stubbornly resilient themselves, vowing to fight a criminal enterprise, and never surrender. They came to see life at its most elementary, yet true. Possessions do not make us who we are. Our dignity is not a reflection of our wealth, or even our home, or popularity. No possessions make us good people, nor things a city.

What makes a city is a sense of place, respect, safety, and acceptance; where we join others in a sense of belonging to something greater than any one of us. What makes a good city is a heritage of trying to find the common good, and people proud to have been a part of the attempt. It is a sense of being somewhere special, with people who care about what stories have been brought forward, and those living next to them today. A city founded on such firm soil of mutual respect will last forever, no matter who or what tries to physically destroy it. It becomes something that cannot die, come murderous criminality, or tornados, or hurricanes. Together we can make our own cities places to be proud of. Together we can make a great city, something to hand on to the next generations.

A CULTURE OF DEATH

A ll speak today of ethics as we do of heaven, as something desirable, but not something real or tangible. We would do well to reconsider. I speak of how ethics determines our fate. The fate of a great empire haunted me when I reflected recently on the Roman Empire. I imagine they, too, believed themselves invincible, but their choices taught them a bitter lesson.

I could not help but be awestruck by the titanic Roman Coliseum. A brooding stone hulk, it dominates the Roman horizon. It is a wonder even today, almost 2,000 years after its construction. A visitor would do well to pause here, at this vast, dead ruin, and consider the end of societies.

We hear much said today about ethics. Ethics in warfare is offered at the U.S. Military Academy at West Point. Scandals remove not only teachers, ministers and captains of industry, but also government and contracting officials as well.

Questionable ethics are pervasive. American civil servants must sign ethics statements; one's word is no longer a bond. We yearn for a remedy, yet the fabric of our nation continues to unravel. Why? Such thoughts crossed my mind as I looked out over the Coliseum's broken chambers, which once held fierce animals and their human victims.

How did Rome, which once civilized the Earth, come to such an end? That whole society, represented by this giant edifice, is gone. I wondered why.

The Roman society that spread throughout the world idealized character. It valued and practiced virtues known even then as peculiar to Rome.

In an essay written about 98 B.C., a Palestinian Jew honored Roman virtues:

"Romans were brave, loyal to their allies, forthright, and without deception. Roman justice was clear and swift. Yet with all this, none of them wore purple or put on a crown as a display of grandeur. They made themselves a Senate house ... deliberating on all that concerned the people and their well being ... and there was no envy or jealousy among them."

Thus a foreigner described republican Rome.

It was a coherent society. Each citizen was honor-bound to do his duties of public service and civil defense. Each tried to behave in the Roman character: to strive for the ideal of the pragmatic, fair and well-balanced citizen. Cincinnatus, a farmer, was called to join his fellow citizens as a soldier to defend Rome from invasion. He left his plow, served and returned, his duty done. The American Minutemen of our Revolutionary War used him as their model of the citizen-soldier. Paul of Tarsus, a Roman citizen, demanded his right to Roman justice in preference to the arbitrariness of other lands. There was no need to teach a Roman duty, honor and country, for such ethical concepts were his everyday life. It was when these common beliefs failed that Rome did, too.

Two Roman legions were annihilated to a man by barbarians in distant, trackless Teutoberg Forest, in what is now Germany. With this disaster, a germ of trouble began. Truths, which inspired Romans to act beyond the call of duty itself, began to fade. Service to the country was no longer considered necessary for pampered, wealthy Roman youths. Rather, the army came to consist of hired foreigners, who worked for pay, not the service of Rome. Virtues that once bound society together became laughable to cynical politicians and profane writers. Even the republic disappeared, and decadent emperors appeared. Virtue was no longer pursued. In its place was substituted the pursuit of pleasure.

The Coliseum was built to satisfy demands for ever more bizarre entertainment. When blood spectacles of gladiators and mass combat no longer thrilled, beasts devouring humans did. Soon, decadent, jaded Romans demanded more. Women were raped by animals. Young slaves were drowned in an artificial lake. Performers were murdered by surprise as they acted. Even whole populations of defenseless Christians and Jews were massacred by perverse methods of crucifixion to amuse Rome. Romans could no longer be shocked.

Salvian, a wise observer, mourned the death of the old ways as he said of his countrymen: "(S)omething still remained to them of their property, but nothing of their character. They reclined at feasts, forgetful of their honor, forgetting justice, forgetting their faith and the name they bore. If my human frailty permitted, I should wish to shout beyond my strength, to make my voice ring through the whole world:

"Be ashamed, ye Roman people everywhere, be ashamed of the lives you lead. Let no one think or persuade himself otherwise - it is our vicious lives alone that have conquered us."

The Coliseum, that vast memorial to folly, stands forever so that what brought Rome down can never be hidden. It proves that a good society survives only by seeking a higher ethic.

Where once Rome was a model of virtue that the world admired, it had become a culture of death. In the quiet of the great Coliseum, I could imagine the whisper of Fate warning us today.

MORALITY PLAY

What began as a Technicolor wonder, of secret meetings, disguises, and devices,

Became a black and white B-grade movie.

Populated by actors who couldn't understand their roles, scripted miles away.

Oh, after all, Ingrid Bergman played best when she didn't know the motive of her character;

Not to say you can't get Oscar winning performances in movies that make little sense.

But why didn't they script the morality play features in at the beginning, before we had to discover them on our own?

Before they ruined so many lives?

And, some never did figure it out.

PAWNS

To fall in love with your source was the gravest sin, of course.

We looked out over our borders every day, with never blinking eyes.

In the aerial view the ground was patch worked; a crazy quilt of haphazard green and brown.

In the planning room, mathematical grid squares replaced the patches.

It all seemed so reasonable, the farther back you were.

Back there, the melancholy river became a blue line; the distant, lonely hill became a three digit number.

Houses became black, two-dimensional squares, not winking lights in the night.

And people? Well, people were sources.

Of significance, they appeared on no map; no grid coordinate indicated their presence.

On the chessboard they were invisible, those pawns.

From the front, we watched, and maneuvered them.

Our binoculars clearly revealed people, with hearts, and breath, and homes, who disappeared into the fog, beyond the river.

I'd spoken to them myself.

It's true, pawns don't speak in a chess match. They are sacrificed for the greater good.

Or so they said, which is why we were not to fall in love with our sources,

Lest we remember them with regret, forever.

A LIFE IN THE THEATER

O ver the theater's portico a bizarre smile beamed down on us. Wholly strange, hauntingly unempathetic; the eyes did not smile.

Was that supposed to be a man's face, or mask, with nothing behind it?

Dozens of statuesque women's physiques, never questioning, ever present, supported the pillars inside.

Never questioning, or warning, of the transfiguration the theater implied.

What you once were will never be the same again; what you once believed will no longer be your bond.

Actors, marionettes, puppets, and wire pullers will be your newfound friends, or cousins, or company men.

And you'll spend your entire life trying to determine which, or if.

Guessing is more productive.

Tromp l'oeil will be your palette; your métier to show convincingly what gets you through today.

Absurdity would thankfully excuse all this, yet there is nothing absurd about off stage mystery, unexpected shots, and secret passages.

Doors to nowhere are real; death is not part of a game, no matter how great.

But then, the play's the thing, after all. You don't have a need to know beyond that.

PERSONAL DELIVERY

In Argentina, in the days of the Generals, one method used by anti-government fighters was to photograph them in their homes, the better to tell them to leave town with their lives.

H e'll never know the 'mailman',

The one who slipped the envelope under his apartment door.

After all, I don't, and I sent him the message.

I imagine him opening the manila envelope, and finding the photograph.

Imagine, the Colonel of interrogation branch, wondering how it happened.

He'll sprint to the bathroom, and look out the window at hundreds of windows, in dozens of buildings.

Any one of them could have held the photographer, the one who shot the photo of his morning shave.

Who could have thought a photograph of a man shaving could cause his heart to race?

Revenge, he raged, on whoever did this!

Revenge, I thought, if you do.

Leave town, Colonel. Leave with your life, an option you didn't offer others.

Or, the next shot will be photographed by the newspapers.

CHANCE ENCOUNTER

Based on the so called "Romeo Spies" of East Germany.

"These were young, handsome men who came to the West and seduced young secretaries who worked for major German politicians and industrialists."

What benign smile of chance brought you to me?

A random turn of the card, and there you were at the Embassy dinner.

Waiting seemed your fate; but then after all you were right

To trust. Wait, and trust.

That evening we shared Austen, then Dickinson at the gazebo;

"Welcome to Vienna," I purred in the rain.

You'd always imagined Bronte's Mr. Rochester with blue eyes,

Just like mine, you said.

Career attained only a secondary clause in our affair,

As you served your beloved Mephistopheles needed, helpful pages from your office

SPECTERS ON A BUS

I dream... the bus arrives at my stop every night, emerging through rain and fog.

Each time I enter, they are all there. Every one. Always.

They sit quietly on either side of the aisle as I pass.

Their eyes look only at me, each in its own way. Erich seems to see me, but looks through me as well.

Karl looks with a certain dread, as if I were a passing specter.

Enigmatically, Hermann and Gunter gaze vacantly, past me into the night.

Only Monika in an indefinable way meets my eyes, as if somehow aware of the entire tale.

But her tears only increased the strange hope she grasped at, even to the end.

Each of the others stare silently as well, fear ridden, in wonder, beyond the pale of anyone's help or caring.

This is what it must have been like at the end for them, all those who trusted.

Where was the line drawn? Was there ever a line, or were they all expendable?

There are more people on the bus, the longer I work.

104

And so my bus comes every night, reminding me there's nowhere off for me, either....

THE COLDEST SEASON

If her ginkgo grew on a university, it would be a quiet rendezvous for young lovers.

Rather it stands by a bench, in a long ago planted grove, crowded now by other, more European trees.

I've watched her here since springtime, with freshets of breeze the only motion in her blonde hair as she reads.

In summer by Sonnenbad she is passed only rarely by walkers, out to enjoy this path by the lake.

Only I see, but am not seen. This abandoned electrical building appears blinded by time.

Yet its window lives.

I know her better than others, since I observe, while others only see.

Her umbrella has two rods, where there should be only one.

Removed, only a natural observer would note it was not a branch, laid next the ginkgo.

She stands, packs her book, adjusts her coat belt, and leaves me; I watch the branch.

A boy comes by, often within a day. He always collects branches.

If noticed at all, one thinks the better of him; keeping his family warm.

106

I see him always retrieve that branch which she left him.

He'll tell us more, but little of value, since he only retrieves and delivers.

She never saw him, but I did.

If it all were different, I could have met her. Only my films now remember those days.

Even now I watch her, on a film by the person I once was; unseen yet there.

I knew her well, and my films helped us know her more.

I watched from the window for the last time … in autumn. The wind blew some leaves by my window, and then I took a walk.

If it were all different... but of course it wasn't. My films betrayed her as much as a kiss.

FLIGHT

*G*enus *Humanus* must deceive

before it can kill.

The lure is relief from fear;

a lulling sense of peace.

Desperate, they broke through the woodline onto a quiet meadow;

Desperate as they burst from a forest fastness

To behold a freshet of water which coursed through open, grassy field;

Leading to a footbridge,

then a little guardhouse.

The red and white crossbar indicated

the frontier station,

And a vanishing line of blue and

white posts the Bavarian border.

West German guards welcomed them

as they collapsed in joy.

Then fresh beer, hearty wursts,

a delirious warm shower, sleep.

Next day they told the Americans

who arrived everything;

Their route, their helpers,

their hopes and dreams.

Only then were they arrested.

The border, a sham; the guards, East Germans;

The Americans, not at all. How could they have known?

They never suspected; their dreams would die first, then their bodies.

MAGIC PEOPLE

Ａnd they wondered how it all worked out the same.

One compromised spy took off for Rome, then disappeared. But not before he sent a charming postcard back from the Eternal City.

Another made it, some few years later, to Marseilles. Then a card to his former boss arrived, 'in all confidence', and then he, too, was gone.

Was it in Helsinki, where the last arrived, only to vanish? And of course the friendly card of "All's well" made it back to base to herald his turning into a puff of smoke.

And another in Munich, and so it went.

And of course, a long time thereafter, they were magically reproduced before cameras in Moscow, denouncing the demons of the West who'd exploited them.

The West?

When they left without a trace, only to reappear speaking of peace-hating Western devils and evil Imperialists; that would pit one set of allies against the other, wouldn't it?

Here was a man, who once worked for the UK, whose "genuine love of peace" made him betray his former employers. So the US would worry about what he'd betrayed that belonged to them.

A clever ploy. And it worked every time. And the card 'home' would light the fuse, causing the allies to fight among themselves, because each would believe one or the other responsible for what went wrong.

Clever?

FRIENDS

The African student was surprised to see the smiling white man plop down on the seat across from him on the northbound 10:35.

Particularly because virtually all the seats were empty, save for one or so, here and there.

A friendly, non-German white man. Was he English?

The newcomer's jovial "Hi there!" greeting showed he was American. Of course. Americans always wanted to talk, unlike the reticent British.

Charming how friendships burst into bloom on casual encounters such as this.

In minutes conversation hopped from jobs, to courses taken, to professors.

Refreshing for a lonely black man at University in a foreign land, to meet someone so kind.

When his station neared, he inquired if the American was able to spare a couple hours, "Would you like to wander my University city for a while? The pedestrian zone is right outside the station."

"Sure!" smiled his guest, after but a flickering moment's hesitation.

Together they walked the outdoor passage on a clear, brisk German day.

Together they chatted, commenting on how such a business, or food, or lady would be seen their own countries.

As the African led the way to his favorite coffee shop in the department store, he turned to find his new friend gone.

The American had vanished in the crowd, the African left wondering what he'd said, or if he was lost.

Had the black man known his real attraction was the man over his shoulder on the train,

And that his new friend disappeared once his replacement surveillant arrived,

He'd be bereft.

As it was, he never knew he was an unwitting cover for surveillance.

 And the prey never suspected an African with a friend would be watching him get off the train, and follow him through town.

As it was, the lonely black man had only the strange story of the vanishing American to tell at home.

IMPORTANCE

We'd passed the memorial so often, I thought it might be nice to stop once and see why it was there.

Placed on the hillside overlooking otherwise valuable wine vineyard country, it had to be important to someone.

I slowed, pulled our car over, and once there my sons jumped out and ran up through the grasses.

As the boys reached the memorial, with me close behind, another car passed by, with young men screaming curses at us and

"Amis 'Raus!"

They wanted us gone, wanted Americans gone, and continued to drive on, continuing their howls into the clear, sunny Weinstrasse day.

Only later did I realize our license plate gave us away; otherwise they might not have cared.

Odd what your memory retains; the boys were too little to remember.

"I KNOW KARATE"

Admittedly, hearing this brought me to tears. As high powered gunfire and screams pierced through the school loudspeaker which someone wisely left on, one little boy told his teacher, "Don't worry, I know karate." This little innocent thought his martial art skills could somehow make the murderer stop. His teacher directed the children where to run, to run literally for their lives to a nearby fire station. The murders in Newtown, Connecticut, show us what we've become. We, as a society, have made this possible.

Whatever the causes, one thing we must do, is become more than this. America has become a place where mass murder is all too common. All too seldom do we attempt to determine if our protections for our young people are enough. We secretly sit and think, Newtown is not our town. And slowly, even this too will fade into the background. We've come to think as long as it isn't us, isn't me, we are all right. Then comes the next horror.

It was in the early 1980's that I attended a class taught by one of the FBI's creators of the unit now known popularly as profilers. He learned that use of a psychiatric evaluation of serial killers reaped great rewards for preventing future killings. Yet even then, all those thirty years ago, at the end of our course he speculated that the 'crime of the future' would be mass shootings. We were left to reflect on that.

Our laws are strange. We rightly prohibit execution of the insane. The ancient 'humanity of English law' prohibits execution for those who, if in their right mind, might offer a defense that would otherwise stay their execution. I believe we should ensure we don't arrive at this juncture. I would suggest that we act beforehand, to prevent our arrival at the controversy of whether or not to execute a man who might be mad.

What we need to do is return to first principles. If evidence suggests a person needs mental health treatment, then he should be sent for help. Interesting we use the word, 'help'. No parent, no community can afford not to evaluate those whose psychiatric condition could lead to violence. We are thus quite literally helping them, because they cannot help themselves. Isn't that what friends do for those needing help in their community? Further, why continue to pretend that those already evaluated as mentally disabled be allowed to 'choose' whether they take their medications or not?. What if the mass murderers we all wring our hands about simply didn't take medication that would have prevented their actions? Is the abstract love of 'privacy' so sacrosanct that we fantasize, or better said, wish, that a person incapable of rational thought be given the 'right' to choose? What if his demons tell him to 'choose' to shoot down little boys and girls in kindergarten?

So, what to do? First, engage mental health professionals in this process. If our goal is to stop mass murderers, and we believe that at least some of them are planned, then meticulously executed, we need to evaluate how this came about. Most would agree that shooting little children in their schools, theater goers, and mall shoppers is not normal. If family members, community representatives, supervisors, or others refer a person for mental health evaluation, then why not a mental health check up, with no repercussions if negative? As a preventive measure, would this not be of value?

What if medication is recommended? Laws which mandate taking such medication would be of great assistance, if only as a preventive measure. But what if treatment is recommended? What if hospitalization? This is the problematic area. A false economic move, defended by specious arguments of privacy and choice, defended closing mental institutions. When we realize that the tremendous success of the FBI's ability to profile serial killers came from interviews of those believed beyond the pale of human value, we need to rethink mental institutions.

A revitalized mental institutional system could be a boon to our society. We would have a vast laboratory of research, the better to understand the human brain, and how to make people well. There, instead of creating vast holding pens for those we don't understand, we could learn how to evaluate, to learn and so to heal.

We owe this to ourselves. We owe trying to stop the next mass murderer to those who visit malls, who go to movies, and to our little children, whose only hope now is whether they "know karate."

REFUGEES DESERVE DIGNITY AND HELP

Who today does not know the "thousand-yard stare?" It is that blank, dead look of animal-like exhaustion in the eyes of soldiers who have seen it all. But I can tell you of a more horrible sight.

Recently I saw a picture of a Balkan woman. She held a pair of brightly colored socks. These socks are local crafts that many Balkan families wear indoors, leaving their shoes at the doorstep. She had made the socks, and now held them for someone with a camera. The socks were the product of a make-work project for refugees from the slaughter in Bosnia.

Horrific were her eyes. They were the eyes of a dead woman. This nameless refugee woman stared right through me. She had the 1,000-yard stare. Was she a mother? Whose daughter was she; whose sister; whose wife? What terrible things had she seen? What had happened to her, to her children, to her husband?

The rainbow-colored socks exhibited a bizarre house of horrors effect: here were works normally associated with pride of craftsmanship, now held by someone who appeared to wish she were dead.

Another refugee said, "I feel that we are increasingly seen as a burden and as a nuisance to society in general and to individuals. They envy us when they see us carry packages with food from the Red Cross and Caritas, but they cannot imagine how humiliating this is for us. They resent the accommodation we are given because they feel we are taking away something that belongs to them, but they have no idea how painful it is to live in someone else's room, lie in someone else's bed, eat at someone else's table.

"Though all that has been given willingly and from the heart, in all my 1,096 days (because when you are a refugee you count each day), I have never been sincerely happy. I feel like a traveler with bags unpacked, a traveler who knows the destination, but the road leading to it is long and uncertain."

This quotation and that picture are from the world we live in today. What are we, as Christians, doing at this Christmas season to help these women as they travel through their circles of hell? We have built great memorials to our war-dead, but I can't help but think that it would be a most terrible sin against them, a mockery of our own fallen and what they fought for, for that better and happier world, not to do something for those in these places of humiliation called refugee camps.

An officer of the First World War offered this, which could be our prayer this Christmas as we remember these violated, tortured women, women who could, but for the love of God, be our own wives:

You smug-faced crowds with kindling eye
Who cheer when soldier lads march by.
Sneak home and pray you'll never know
The hell where youth and laughter go.

Remember the eyes with the 1,000-yard stare. They are counting the days. Swear that you'll never forget.

FIGHTING WITH PRAYERS AND CANDLES

"I have been driven many times to my knees by the overwhelming conviction that I had nowhere to go. My own wisdom, and that of all about me, seemed insufficient for the day." Abraham Lincoln

On the tiny square near the church of St. Nikolas (the Nikolaikirche) in formerly Communist Leipzig, Germany, stands a strange monument. It is a brilliantly white Doric pillar topped by carved, pale green palms. I read that it commemorated the actual site where the peaceful revolution began the revolution that in time brought down Communism.

More importantly, it brought into high relief for me two conflicting world views. On one side was the materialist worldview. It held, as the East German dictator Eric Honecker said, "The German Democratic Republic doesn't need churches."

The other viewpoint was represented by a story that happened at the small, brown-brick Nikolaikirche. This unprepossessing building was where a Monday evening prayer service began in 1981. The prayers were for world peace. When I entered the quiet church last year, it seemed so normal. People prayed; visitors came and went. Its interior, delineated by Doric pillars capped by strangely beautiful, intricately carved, pale green acanthus leaves, was remarkably peaceful. The visitor can hardly imagine what it was like however, when one's very presence was noted by secret police, or "Stasi" informers. Once, public prayer was considered so much superstition by the Communist government, and was to be contained only within church walls, there to be eyed by the ubiquitous "Stasi". As long as believers remained docile, such time-wasting was allowed. Fear of surveillance and arrest controlled people's lives. One young woman told me that her father, a minister, knew his phone was tapped his entire life.

Over time the Monday evening peace prayers unaccountably grew in popularity. The gray lifestyle of materialist East Germany could never answer a hunger for a spiritual life. One who sought a spiritual dimension inevitably became a heretic against the Communist viewpoint. Many Americans find it hard to believe that once someone actively practiced Christianity, they fell afoul of the only authority that could grant higher education, jobs, apartments, cars, or any other material benefits. Fear prevailed. A practicing Christian could lose his job, could compromise his child's future, or could find himself and his family in prison.

Throughout the decade of the 1980's the strange events in the Nikolai-kirche grew more apparent; the pews were filled to overflowing. Listeners crowded the doors to hear about a peace beyond all understanding, about comfort for those who mourn, about Christ who counseled, "Fear not."

The Communists reacted with naked power. Arrests followed. Yet still more listeners came. Word of mouth about the peace prayers of Monday night at the church took on an otherworldly dimension. People came from Dresden and far away Berlin. The Communist leadership ordered hundreds of their members to pack the church in order to block regular attendance. I found myself smiling at the idea of the minister given the opportunity to preach to a church full of convinced Communists about reconciliation and the spiritual dimension of life. Clearly God has a sense of humor!

With the passing weeks young "Volkspolizei", or "People's Police" were sent to cordon off the crowds spilling out onto the square. A wise pastor encouraged everyone to hold a candle as a symbol of solidarity and peacefulness. Because one needs two hands to hold a candle, he has no hand free to cause violence. Someone began a chant, "We are the people!" The people naturally pressed against the helmeted, faceless police. I saw this with my own eyes in confiscated Stasi surveillance films of this very event.

Soon the people simply walked around them, and the young men fell back. The church assembly wended its way out of the square, through the narrow streets and on to the massive Karl Marx Platz. Peacefully they flowed, now in the thousands, some mothers pushing baby carriages, around the city ring road chanting, "We are the people!" As they neared the dreaded Stasi headquarters, they began to simultaneously shout, "Shame on you! Shame on you!" As a Communist party chief lamented, "We planned for everything. We were ready for everything...except prayers and candles." As I learned the story I was overwhelmed with living evidence of the power of prayer.

In the end, prayers and candles brought down the Wall, and then European Communism. When I visited the Nikolaikirche I reflected on what kept people coming, despite all the guns, police and jails arrayed against them. What gave them the strength to carry on? I'll never forget, as I wandered through the sanctuary area, that the Bible was open on a podium to a text that read, "Fear not."

SECRET LETTER WRITER

Each curve of the unknown hand, each rounded letter revealed the message.

Words only enlarged the enticement, so finely were they crafted.

Who could but envy one so enamored, if only to wish her for his own?

Yet now the secret message was known by all who were authorized to read it.

Every cipher clerk who transmitted the memo before it was 'sent' smiled, or day-dreamt of another

Wishing she could write so well, or so meaningfully.

It was scripted by someone called "Rochelle", whose existence, like her love,

Was only taken off a tombstone, where until needed, had rested in peace.

AFGHANISTAN'S WANDERERS

Until I met Shokria, I had never met anyone from Afghanistan. My family then lived in the Netherlands. It was through a Dutch friend that we were introduced to Shokria, Muslim mother of three boys, nurse, war refugee, and our neighbor. Her English was the broken remnant of classes given twenty years ago in far away Kabul, Afghanistan, by an intrepid Peace Corps volunteer. It was sufficient to tell us this story.

Shokria was married to Aziz, a flower seller in the Afghani capital of Kabul. Flowers play a significant role in any Afghani activity, lending color to a hardy, tough life. One day, police installed by the Soviet/Afghan Communist government arrested Aziz at his shop. At the time we met Shokria in Holland, no one knew where Aziz was or if he was alive. No one was even sure why he was arrested. He had been gone over a year in the shadow land of the Communist prison system. That, of course, is one of the means of control in the tyranny. No one is ever sure what the law is, so no one is ever sure if he has violated it or not.

Shokria's father gathered up the family fortune and helped her and her children escape over the Khyber Pass to Pakistan. From there he secured them passage to Holland. It was the Dutch government that provided Shokria and her children refuge, an apartment, a stipend and Dutch language lessons.

When we first met, it was the rare occasion that Shokria's story did not end with her in tears of frustration, sorrow and terror. Where was her husband? Was he even alive? What had happened to her father and the rest of her family?

By law, she could not work, for refugees could take no Dutch job. She could not travel, for she had no passport. That was now in the possession of the Dutch government, and in fact she had no money to do so anyway. She had nowhere to go. She could not call her country because of the war. The Communists controlled all the Afghan embassies. She could only sit and wait. But what, in fact, was she waiting for? The wait was maddening, because the wait could last forever. Shokria seemed to be sinking deeper and deeper into that alien land and culture.

We wrote to Amnesty International. We hoped to find out if there was a way to determine her husband's fate. A very thorough and caring correspondent replied that there was a way, through the International Red Cross. Shokria's reaction to this news was not what we expected. She feared that a by-name inquiry would bring revenge and torture upon her husband, if he lived. We assured her it would not; that the inquiries would be discreet and general. Shokria was so terrified for her husband that she could not pursue this method.

Then it dawned on me. We live in a world where the police are there to protect us, where the jails are for the criminals. Of course the reassurances of international organizations are sufficient for us, but not for Shokria, without a homeland, and only her children to physically reassure her of the goodness of the way things were, before her world disappeared.

The treatment she was dealt by some of her Dutch neighbors was shameful. They resented her protections, reminding her that they, taxpayers, paid for it all; that she had no right to anything. The bureaucrat who serviced her 'case' only made certain that she did not work, pointing out that her degree meant nothing in Holland. Shokria whirled down and down in the quicksand which an uncertain fate creates.

As luck would have it, in an obscure bookstore, my wife found a book entitled, "A Trip to Mecca," a book about the Muslim holy city. In it were Islamic prayers written in Arabic, a language Shokria could read. For the first time Shokria cried with joy. She prayed daily for her husband's deliverance. The next we heard from Shokria she was ecstatic. Her husband Aziz was alive and free. He had been expelled from Afghanistan in a general, unexplained release of prisoners. The reunion of the family in Holland was one of our happiest memories. Our two families feasted together on lamb, rice and vegetables, the staples of that far away land of Afghanistan. It was the ancient sense of celebration!

Aziz had been tortured, and I saw the horrific marks. He never knew why he had been arrested, and he never knew why he had been released. Shokria and her family still wait in Holland. In comparison, of course, they are among the lucky of the faceless millions of unseen refugees among us. They are materially secure. That would, of course, be sufficient if we were only material creatures, without feelings, dreams, hopes or loves.

Sometimes the best we can do for others is what we'd hope they'd do for us if fortunes were reversed. Imagine yourself lonely, and in need of a friend.

BUILDING FREEDOM

"Am I not destroying my enemy when I make friends of them?" Abraham Lincoln

Our pilgrimage to Czechoslovakia began when my family and I drove across the Iron Curtain. The 1989 Velvet Revolution that displaced the Communists had only recently concluded. A heady, strange, but exciting mood seemed to permeate the very air.

As the country quietly prepares to dissolve this week into independent Czech and Slovak states, I've thought often about that trip. I want to tell you about four people we met there.

First, though, our destination. After trip arrangements Byzantine in complexity, we finally reached our vacation house in a tidy town in forested, ancient Bohemia. The name Bohemia, for most Americans, conjures up associations as exotic and unfamiliar as the Holy Roman Empire or the magical kingdom of Avalon. In fact, this was part of the former Sudetenland, the Germanic district of Czechoslovakia.

It was to annex the Sudetenland that Hitler invaded the country in 1938. No Germans live there now, having been driven away in 1945 with the war's end. Because of this connection, though, I hoped to find people I could talk to. (I speak German, but no Czech.) I was dying to know what it was like to live there during the Iron Curtain years. Luck follows my travels. Our vacation home was in one of these quaint old German towns. We were the very first guests of remarkably kind Czech hosts.

Until only a few years earlier no one had been allowed to live in the area, for this was the former No Man's Land. It was the land emptied of people and farms to provide a militarized security zone of gun towers, machine-gun pillboxes and minefields to control the border with the West.

What had been the jewel of European kingdoms past, with bountiful harvests, bulging barns, plump cattle and prosperous communities, was allowed to become forest and scrub. Wolves in the wild had returned.

Slowly, with the Cold War's stagnation, some of the dilapidated houses were made available for purchase and restoration by Czechs. We stayed in such a house. In time, my hope to learn of life there began to be realized. A bookseller told us what she remembered. "I was a little girl of six in 1945. I remember when the American Army liberated our village. A black soldier would come to my window every morning and give me a piece of gum. We never had gum before," she said. "Then one day the Americans left and the Russians arrived. "Years later, when I was in the third grade, our teacher would ask us to recite the answer to, 'Who liberated our village?' I answered, 'the Americans'", the bookseller said. "My teacher became very angry because I didn't say the Soviet Red Army". She was stubborn, "because I knew what I knew. My mother was called to the school to explain my behavior. She was told that she would lose her job and that I would be expelled if I did not answer 'correctly'. 'Do you want me to tell my daughter to lie?' my mother asked. In time, I said that the Red Army liberated us."

Another Czech woman, married to a car mechanic, remembered how in the 1980s she became fascinated by what life must be like beyond the Iron Curtain, in the West. After years of applications, investigations and general harassment by Czechoslovakian Communist bureaucrats she and her husband were allowed to visit her sister who had defected to West Germany. But they were allowed to take the equivalent of only $20 out of the country for their "vacation."

The couple was struck by the differences between East and West. "We only drove around. It was so colorful in the West. People came and went as they pleased. Everyone seemed to smile and laugh. People would greet you. We saw marvelous automobiles," the woman said.

"The stores had simply everything. We could only afford to sleep in our car. We were ashamed to go anywhere because we were so poorly dressed. My sister gave me a large box of wonderful soap powder to take home as a souvenir." She smiled at this, then continued her story.

"When we came back to the Czechoslovakian border we were made to wait in our car six hours until 2 a.m.," she said. "Then we were taken into separate interrogation rooms by Czech border police. They demanded a complete written summary of our trip." Their car was pulled apart and they were strip-searched. "The police matron asked me, while I stood there naked, what I had brought back with me. I told her that the soap powder was all," the woman told us. "She tore open the box, scooped through it with her hand, pouring it out in handfuls all over the table. Then she shoved the half-empty box at me. 'Get dressed and get out!' I cried the rest of the way home."

There were more stories of repression.

The Sunday during our visit to Czechoslovakia happened to be Easter. After church services we went to talk to the local pastor. He was a younger, quite friendly fellow. He seemed to have 16 appointments simultaneously, as do pastors everywhere. "The Lord's calling me to the ministry had to be answered secretly," he said. "I studied secretly under the instruction of an old priest. No one in the factory where I worked could know. Not even my parents knew." That way, if he was arrested they wouldn't be involved. "My clandestine ordination was the happiest day of my life. Now I am happy to follow my calling in the open, in a normal way," he said.

The former airbase in the area was now offering sightseeing flights on planes once used to fly surveillance along the border. An energetic pilot, Lazio, took a liking to my sons, Will and Kenny. "Come on boys. Let's take a special flight in this Zlin," he said, pointing to a single-engine, four-seater Piper-Cub type plane. Most parents don't get the chance to see their boys in a plane executing Stuka-type dives, breath-taking arcs and magnificent "swooshes," for want of a better word. And most of them probably could live without knowing it was one of their boys at the controls during such wild airborne antics.

But the boys had an exhilarating, free and happy ride, given by a pilot who loved sharing his love of flying. "That was the greatest time of my life!" was the assessment of our 11-year-old, Kenny.

That evening we sat by the fireplace of our temporary home in Bohemia. My oldest son Marty talked about a young girl he'd met who said, "After our Velvet Revolution, everything seemed so new. It is all so different from what I've been taught all through school. I don't know what truth is now."

It seemed a strangely deep observation for a young girl who was forced to grow up almost overnight, from the dark "one truth" world of communism into a kaleidoscope of opinions and options. It seemed to me that people who emerge from gloom after so long, who can now speak openly to anyone, even to foreigners, have no need to fear the future.

Czechs need no longer fear the crazy robot system, supported by thugs, which made war on third-graders, persecuted soap-powder owners and made it a crime to learn about God. The strange, heady feeling we sensed during our Bohemian adventure was freedom.

Freedom isn't only about abstracts like liberty. Freedom is the chance to turn a deserted ruin into a vacation home, to smile at strangers and to give a little boy the airplane ride of his life.

GOD'S GRACE AND SCHINDLER

"Nobody ever made a greater mistake than when he did nothing because he could only do a little." Edmund Burke, British Parliamentarian

Oscar Schindler lied. He seduced women. He exploited his Nazi friends and party membership for profit. Schindler drank, smoked, and traded shamelessly on the black market. Yet I use him as a model in religion classes. Why?

With the movie "Schindler's List" now on television, the strange case of Oscar Schindler is once again in the news. Editorials and movie reviews conclude that Schindler is incomprehensible. His actions are alien to any of today's relativist behavioral norms.

Here was a Nazi who saved Jews. Why, they ask? What motivated him? A favored term for Schindler analysts, after careful appraisal of his character, is that he is "morally ambiguous." I think this means they haven't a clue why Oscar Schindler behaved the way he did. For Christians however, the answer is clear, even obvious. Oscar Schindler was touched by grace.

Schindler was a manipulator and hedonist. An opportunist, he insinuated himself into a profitable venture in expropriated and plundered Krakow, Poland. A war profiteer, he contracted some 1,300 Jewish workers at no pay. But sometime after he established his Polish factory, God knocked at his heart. Then Schindler, a seemingly typical amoral man of the Nazi New World Order, responded to God's invitation. It would not be an easy choice. Was it not Jesus who counseled that those who chose to follow him would be like sheep among the wolves; that they must be soft as lambs, but sharp as serpents?

Schindler, to do good, had to continue living surrounded by evil. It is interesting to note that about the time of Schindler's conversion, St. Maximilian Kolbe, a Polish Franciscan, was condemned to death in Auschwitz extermination camp, only a few miles from Krakow.

Kolbe commented in a letter written in 1932 that " . . .every person has the makings of a saint. Each person, assigned a mission by God, is born with the abilities proportionate to that mission, and throughout each person's whole life, the environment, circumstances, and everything else contribute to make it possible to accomplish that mission."

Schindler had deserted God, but God had not deserted him. Like Mary Magdalene, Schindler was lost to sin and vice. But then God mysteriously offered another way, and Schindler accepted. Secretly, he answered the quiet but persistent tug of grace and the Holy Spirit. But how could he do good in the horrible hell of the Third Reich?

As Kolbe observed, "Besides natural gifts, every person is also accompanied by the grace of God from the cradle to the tomb. God's grace is poured on each of us in such quantity and quality that our weak human nature strengthens itself by acquiring the supernatural energy we need to face our own mission."

It would require a great grace to wrench good from a miasma of death camps, machine guns and hate. But God is stronger than hate, stronger than wolves. Through the action of grace, Schindler found the strength for his clandestine battle with Nazidom. What happened? Consider the evidence.

Schindler fed the hungry. The "Schindler Juden" (Schindler Jews) were always adequately fed with food he adroitly acquired for them on the black market. He did this while other Jews were being systematically starved in the ghettos.

He clothed the naked. He finessed decent clothing for Jews who had been forced to run naked before Nazi 'doctors' who selected them for work or death.

He gave drink to the thirsty. Schindler duped Nazi guards into watering down death trains where midsummer heat tortured those packed inside.

He visited the imprisoned; he saved those meant to be murdered. He bribed everyone who stood between him and those for whom he had a mission. He did this despite all the laws, guns and police of Hitler's empire.

As a consequence of Schindler's chicanery, bribery and double-crossing of the Nazis, he was able to comfort the afflicted and wretched Jews in ways unimaginable. Each day, during four years of war, Oscar Schindler risked his life for the least of his brethren, the Jews. The Jews, considered by Nazis as things to be killed, became the Chosen People delivered by this unlikely Moses.

How did he do it? How did Schindler, in the very belly of the Nazi beast, do it? Schindler used his dubious natural talents of a ready wit, a smooth tongue and well-practiced bonhomie to delude even psychopathic, fanatical Nazis. But moreover he cooperated with God's supernatural gifts and so saved the Jews in his care. He did God's will.

I read "Schindler's List" in 1981 while stationed in Germany. I was very disappointed to learn that he died an impoverished unknown some five years earlier in Frankfurt. I believe that someday I'll get to meet Oscar Schindler. What he did for the least of his brothers, he did for Christ. I suspect he entered into a happier place prepared for him.

DRESDEN ARISE

"Truth never damages a cause that is just."-Mahatma Gandhi."

The Venetian artist Canaletto painted the magnificent panorama of Dresden, Germany, in the 18th century. The artist sat across the Elbe River to record what even then was known as the "Florence of the North." Dresden was a cultural city. Augustus the Strong, King of Saxony whose capital was Dresden, surrounded himself with architectural wonders. Canaletto's view encompassed the wondrous cityscape. To his right was the Hofkirche, or Court Church, the Jesuit marvel in white on the square. There too was the baroque Zwinger, Augustus' flamboyant royal palace. Further left and upriver came the Bruhlsche Terrasse gardens, the Balcony of Europe, replete with ranks of shade trees lined against the magnificent Albertinum. The latter building, with the names of great artists etched in stone, contained jewels and artistic treasures that made Dresden a required stop for any educated traveler of the Grand Tour era. There also were the ponderous casements and the light and colorful Renaissance Georgenbau. The walkways linking these distinct masterpieces of masonry, stone and brick created a symphony of craftsmanship that welcomed guests as they approached across the Elbe river.

Overwhelming all of this was the leftmost anchor of the panorama, the huge cupola of the Frauenkirche. This looming, majestic Evangelical Lutheran church completed a harmonious aria of man's construction. Where the Hofkirche seemed to point upward to God, the Frauenkriche suggested the return of God's omniscient blessing, apparent in its tremendous cupola.

In 1945, another arc was drawn over the cityscape of Dresden. Using the Deutsche Sport Club stadium as the pivot, a compass line was drawn that embraced the entire city center. The lines were on a British aerial photograph used to target the city for a terror bombing mission. This map still exists as an exemplar of modern war.

On the night of Feb. 13-14, 1945, after marking flares were dropped to square off the target area, flights of several hundred British bombers struck. A phenomenon known as a firestorm was created. Flames sucked all the oxygen from the affected area, suffocating even those in bunkers.

One woman recalled that all the imprisoned women at a labor camp near the city center were killed either by high explosives, flame, or suffocation. Among the victims was her mother, who was arrested for refusing to divorce her Jewish husband imprisoned in Buchenwald. Over 100,000 Germans perished in the inferno of Dresden, together with the architectural masterpieces that Canaletto knew.

A haunting black and white photograph, taken the day after the bombing from behind a charred sandstone statue of a woman, seems to suggest "behold Apocalypse." Her outstretched arm reveals miles of randomly piled masonry, chimneys, and empty frames that once were homes, palaces, museums, and an opera hall. The massacre was total and horrific.

A visitor today can sit where once Canaletto did, and see virtually what he saw. The actual location is indicated, and from there the panorama looks much as it did in the 18th Century. Indeed, not only have the Zwinger, the Hofkirche, and the Georgenbau been carefully restored, but the incredible Semper Opera, built since the painting, also graces the vast public space near the Zwinger. These wonders are wholly restored. The most memorable of art museums, with Raphael's Sistine Madonna as the crowning work of its collections, awaits the viewer. In every corner there are quaint coffee shops, cultural exhibits, artisans, music, and museums. This is a walker's city, which beckons with its fountains, restored public buildings, and theaters, not to mention its Grosser Garten, a truly remarkable park.

Moreover, Dresden is a river city. The "white fleet" of river steamships dock at the harbor. If this nautical prospect seems to betoken another age, there is a reason. These ships, each of which is sleekly built to the demanding standards of yesteryear, date in some cases to the 1880s!

The arc of one's view of modern Dresden today would not be complete without the story of that last great building construction, the mammoth Frauenkirche, Our Lady's Church. In regimented cases stacked all around, huge blocks of stone, rescued from the ruins of the original building, were marked and ranked for placing in the edifice. In a welcome center nearby, one could watch the construction via cameras placed inside the work space. Notable too were the displays about the Dresden reconstruction funds, to which people around the world, especially from the United Kingdom, have contributed. Indeed, a former Dresdener gave his Nobel Prize award to this huge civic project. The now completed construction effort alone would be worth a visit, but there is another dimension, at once more touching as well as inspiring.

The titanic base of the church, during its rebuilding, was sheathed in protected scaffolding against the weather while work continued. Over these protective coverings were placed two immense placards. "Brücken bauen. Versohnung leben." "Build Bridges. Live Reconciliation." These ideas acknowledge that the past cannot be changed, but the future can. Reconciliation can heal. Dresden wants to become again not only a world cultural center, but a city of world peace, with the Frauenkirche as a place of international reconciliation.

With the Frauenkirche finished, one can now again see the whole panorama that Canaletto once saw and know that the dreams of millions for peace founded upon reconciliation are realized in this edifice. A huge golden cross displayed in the church is a copy of the one which was once on top of the Frauenkirche, the one that Canaletto saw. It was made by an English goldsmith, whose father was a bomber pilot on that Ash Wednesday night in February, 1945.

"Brücken Bauen. Versohnung Leben."

TORTURE BREAKS EVERYONE, INCLUDING THE TORTURERS

In the center of the empty concrete room squatted a single, ancient, wooden bathtub. The museum director who placed it there knew the power the tub conveyed. It was the actual tub used by the Gestapo in Den Haag, the Netherlands, as an interrogation device during World War II. The prisoner was strapped to a board, then held under the water until he thought he was going to drown. It was that simple.

In Krakow, Poland, there is a nondescript building that sits on a side street corner. It is known as the Silesian House. It was there that the Gestapo set up its initial interrogation cells. Taken naked into this dungeon, for its cells were underground, a prisoner would be brought into one cell where a wooden device shaped like two x's connected by a central axis awaited her. There was no description of how this apparatus was used. It was left to your imagination.

One prisoner commented that as he was taken to that room, he saw a naked woman suspended head down from the ceiling of another cell. The human imagination in such cases was very effective. When stories of such a place "leaked out" to the larger city's population, fear and horror wove its way through the public mind. It was a form of terrorism. Such was intended to keep the occupied nation under control. Such methods -- tying women naked to ceilings and near-drowning -- were ultimately intended to save German soldiers' lives by revealing future Resistance attacks. The Nazis actually called these attacks terrorism.

There seems to be a debate today about what is considered torture. Much of the controversy centers on whether it "works." Such a mechanistic appraisal is very American. We are, after all, a practical nation. We like our computers to work, our airplanes to fly on time. We like our coffee to be hot when served. Anything, some argue, is authorized if it "saves one American life." This is, for many, a compelling argument.

There was another aspect of this argument, though, which I remember quite well from my visits to that chilling Dutch museum and terrifying Polish cell.

It was a quotation from a resistance fighter. He said, as I recall, that it was the sheer dread of the Gestapo members that made him decide to join the fight against them. His utter disgust at Gestapo methods hinted, rumored or actually used was enough for him to secretly do what he could to bring down the Nazi order. He hated them with a black passion that was not deterred by the fear. The fear made him, and thousands of others, join the fight against the Nazis. Who, then, was saved by the methods used?

Just last month, in Washington, D.C, a great secret of World War II was revealed. The Army commemorated a secret band of American interrogators from that war. For some 65 years, they kept the secret of their incredible success at interrogating Nazis at little-known Fort Hunt, which lies just outside our capital. These men, who "broke" the Nazi generals and scientists brought to them, did so without using any controversial techniques. Indeed, they are outspoken in their denunciation of such methods as water boarding, and they do not want their successes' recognition in any way to appear to justify today's methods.

The Washington Post quotes 90-year-old Henry Kolm, a physicist at MIT: "We got more information out of a German general with a game of chess or Ping-Pong than they do today, with their torture."

These elderly men, whose interrogations in some degree literally helped win World War II, all denounce torture, pure and simple. They have no problem recognizing it and calling it what it is.

And they, perhaps more than anyone, know another, deeper reason to avoid the use of torture. They know what it can do to the torturer, too. Perhaps most powerful was 87-year-old George Frenkel's comment: "During the many interrogations, I never laid hands on anyone. We extracted information in a battle of the wits. I'm proud to say I never compromised my humanity."

Whether a system "works" in the short term never considers its effect on the man or woman required to apply it. The torturer is marked forever, with Macbeth-like blood which only they can see. They become secret sociopaths, alcoholics, drug users or worse. They do so to make the pain go away, if only for a while, because the memories never do.

I often wonder why two Germans I met confessed to me their awareness of such practices. One described a chance encounter with a former classmate who told him in a drunken rage in 1942 how "we are shooting them all" in torture fields of Poland. Another suffered in postwar years under a father whose drunken rampages displaced, at least for him if not for his child, the wartime interrogations he conducted in the Ukraine and Holland.

What 22-year-old American soldier and his yet-to-be-born children will suffer as well someday, the same way? We may even know him. How will today's interrogators be recognized someday for their work? Will they seek comfort in fine words, such as those spoken by CIA Chief Michael Hayden?

Hayden, when directly asked if water boarding was torture and whether the United States would continue to use it, answered: "Judge (Michael) Mukasey (attorney general nominee) cannot nor can I answer your question in the abstract. I need to understand the totality of the circumstances in which this question is being posed before I can give you an answer."

The men who interrogated Nazis at Fort Hunt would have no problem answering that question. They know what torture is.

We can be proud of our men at Fort Hunt. They never compromised their humanity. The men at Fort Hunt helped reveal secret German weapons programs, strategies and plans. Their Nazi enemies were at least as brutal as those who confront us today. Our men overcame them with intelligence, not bestiality.

It has been said evil men are always amazed that good people can be clever, too.

These members of "the Greatest Generation" seemed to grasp intuitively that torture creates enemies. It doesn't stop them.

Torture breaks everyone involved. No amount of double-talk makes the pain go away.

If neither the head of the CIA nor the prospective attorney general can say categorically that water boarding is torture, we have crossed an eddy of the river of no return.

Torture kills souls. The only cure for such spiritual pain is confession.

THE FAREWELL

L ong trips through the countryside avail nothing, without the warmth of a human embrace.

Trust comes only with the charming Gasthaus, where an intimate dinner over friendly asides about music, shared experiences of appreciated wines, bind.

So grows confidence, so a trust that draws together even more.

So even the simple promise, a kindness...to honor a new friend's request.

So even the private meeting, where no one knows but you two.

Like lovers. Yes, like lovers who stand outside the conflict that brought you together.

Whose care for one another only wants to help bring the joy of shared love to others, who cannot, but must, see the love that has grown, even here.

For did love not happen to you both, you who were professional enemies?

And yet, though no one remembers, Aeneas betrayed Dido, so why not you, too?

Who do you long for when the next meeting is not with the beloved, but jack-booted thugs?

You'll spend your remaining hours knowing it wasn't him. There was some mistake.

BERLIN AGAIN

In my mind's eye I saw the Brandenburg Gate rising above an eerily lit no-man's land. That Neo-Classical symbol of Berlin rose above a flat landscape punctuated with East German guard towers, leashed, hungry, man-hunting dogs, and young men carrying machine pistols. It was demarcated of course by the relentless, soul-killing, Berlin Wall. Yet my memory of nineteen years ago was truly and utterly challenged by my visit to the new Berlin this month.

My wife and I celebrated our 25th wedding anniversary with a pilgrimage of sorts. We wanted to see what life was like in a land we once knew as a young married couple. Berlin then was two cities. One was Western, bright, and self-consciously bulging with material goods. This was perhaps best characterized by Ka-De-We, the Kaufhaus des Westens. This incredible place, a store on a par with Harrod's of London, encapsulated the economic success of the West. Here you could find Givenchy, Rolex, Italian shoes, and every other wonder of Western material choice and wealth. Ka-De-We's food department literally reveled in excess of wines, cheeses, and every food known to man. It was, so far as I could tell, the only place outside Africa where one could find tiger meat!

Berlin in those days was still under the four Allied Powers' jurisdiction. Indeed, I could ride all public transportation free of charge if I wore my uniform. To visit the eastern side of Berlin, however, required participation in an "official tour". There we saw the dismal legacy of Communist dictatorship. We saw apartment buildings through which daylight flashed between poorly mortared pre-fab segments, 'stores' which carried cheaply made imitations of imagined Western items, bookstores replete with Communist theology, rare cafeterias and souvenir shops which shamed even the salespeople, and of course the inevitable sad, long, lines of people waiting for whatever was available. I remember putting back a little toy bear I found in a 'toy department', since clearly it was the only one. We were aware that some child in the East would not have it if we took it home. Was the color of the city then really so gray?

Police surveillance was everywhere. Little men in black trench coats or cheap suits obviously latched onto our 'suspect' Western group at every stop. These were the secret police, the only people who would look us in the eye. The average citizen of that benighted police state avoided any "West contact", which was immediately noted and reported. Indeed, we were cautioned not to speak to average citizens, since they would later be interrogated by the ubiquitous Communist plainclothesmen. Significantly, a huge "socialist realism" mural above the famed Alexanderplatz revealed an all-seeing camera under the outstretched arm of a scientist pointing the way to the Orwellian "great socialist future." A souvenir shop surveilled purchasers with cameras hidden behind baskets. In St. Hedwig's Cathedral I saw little men take names of worshippers, thus to remind them that their expression of faith would cost them dearly.

But that was then, some twenty years ago. Today, there is none of that. I repeat for emphasis, none. I could hardly orient myself due to the absolutely massive construction effort in virtually every single part of downtown Berlin. My wife Jane actually felt physically dizzy when we emerged from the smooth, rapid, clean, and extraordinarily efficient subway system onto the Potsdamerplatz. We were surrounded by the twenty-first century's most wondrous architectural accomplishments. Sony, IMAX, Mercedes, and every scientific advance known to man's technical genius are now physically represented here. There is a three-score floor building with the fastest elevator on earth (To the top in 20 seconds! I wonder where some of our rocket science has gone!) The flat fields for Communist cross-fire are no more. Indeed, there is such a complete **Vernichtung**, such a thoroughgoing elimination, of any vestige of the Wall that I wondered if there was ANY representation still present. In fact one can still visit "Checkpoint Charlie", an anachronism located in a bustling section of town that was once forbidding and grey. Those empty fields of yesteryear are today's prime Berlin real estate. Those fields now house hyper-modern telecommunications buildings, stations which service whisper-quiet Intercity trains, and a host of other architectural marvels. Double-decker buses roam everywhere and on time, and the once dilapidated S-Bahn city train is a smooth carpet of transit.

Mighty public buildings of the new German capital are housed in either hyper-sanitized high-rises or authentically rebuilt Prussian edifices. Walking down the famed Unter-den-Linden one feels as if he is in the last century. Great care and expense have gone into refurbishing brooding Humboldt University, the Crown Prince's Palace, and the City Opera House. In this twenty first century city, a true sense of the past will be preserved for all time. Magnificent housing for the city's cultural heritage will be maintained with the complete rebuilding, according to the original plans, of the great city museums. The Museum Island's Bode, Pergamum (site of the like-named Athenian altar carvings), and Old German museums (with its world-class Greek and Roman sculptures, and 19th Century art collections) are but a few of the dozens of historical buildings being restored to their former magnificence. The museums will be connected by an underground passage that will link every one of the former Prussian Royal Collections so that even on rainy days the visitor will be able to enjoy the plethora of items in total comfort. Consider too, however, that with reunification virtually all the art of empires past, from the Kaiser's to the Weimar periods, and even modern collections are now available for view without political ramifications. This massive assemblage of art demanded more space, and the new Berlin has given it with the incredibly huge Kultureforum. There no less than a half dozen major museums of paintings, (Van Eyck and every famous name you can remember from Art History class), prints, applied arts, and more sit among theaters, symphony halls, and every cultural activity your heart desires.

Berlin does not deny its past. What then, of the calamity that brought all this about? There will be a tremendous, monumental- in-size memorial to the millions of Jews murdered by the Third Reich only two blocks from the very center of Berlin. Significantly, it will be within eyesight of the Reichstag, the German Parliament, thus to remind the lawmakers who must not forget. Likewise, Bebelplatz on Humboldt University, the place where Nazis burned "decadent" books, is commemorated for all time. A quote in bronze by the great German writer Heinrich Heine, written in 1820, overlooking a memorial of bare bookshelves, symbolically links the two events when he wrote, " They who start by burning books will end by burning people."

What did it all mean, after all, for two sojourners from the Cold War seeking a sort of catharsis? This pulsing, powerful, and wonderful; this culturally sensitive yet mega-modern city, was nothing like the one we once knew. We sought a sort of balance, an assessment. Yesterday's gray functionaries and their police state mentality were replaced by sculpted-haired, cell-phoned, laptop equipped young technocrats near ranks of Mercedes aligned around the refurbished, titanic Reichstag. What did it all mean?

It was hard to assess the material wealth being poured into the city. Billions of German Marks will turn sleepy Berlin-Schönefeld Airport into the last word in aviation technology. Contrast that with the lovingly rebuilt Berliner Dom and St. Hedwig's Cathedral, the two great churches near the Brandenburg gate. These were open and people freely worshipped in them. One of the ironies of the Cold War era lives on, however. In the 1970's the money given by Western churches to rebuild the neglected Eastern churches damaged in the Second World War was stolen by the Communist government to build the huge downtown television tower. When the sun strikes it, the largest cross on earth is created on its rounded, mirrored dome. All the efforts of Communist architecture to erase this phenomenon failed, and the so-called "Pope's Revenge" still sparkles over Berlin on any sunny day.

Yet the Wall was gone, and with it the largest part of my past experience. We sought to find our past somehow, and journeyed to the place on Bernauerstrasse where we looked over the wall on a sad, rainy day so many years ago. We sought the giant Gothic church that once stood there. It was then surrounded by two ranks of the Berlin Wall in no man's land. We remembered the apparent metaphor of that abandoned, lonely, empty church trapped between the walls and patrol roads on the other side. Tragically we learned that the church was blown up by Communist authorities in 1985, only a few years after our visit. Officially it was to give a clearer field of fire for their "anti-fascist defensive wall", but in reality it was because several people escaped, using the church as a hideout. Only four years later the Wall came down, and with it the physical structure which protected a miasma of lies. The new church is a much smaller, simpler, modern structure of poured concrete to symbolize its past association with the Wall. The cross over it is the bent, wrought-iron one of the old church which flew into the West when the church was dynamited. Inside, behind the altar is a carved "Last Supper", likewise rescued from the old church. The faces of Jesus and several disciples are smashed, the legacy of bored East German guards who used the old sanctuary for rest-breaks.

As we left the church, we found what perhaps answered our own questions of the meaning of this visit to Berlin. There at the entrance was a statue which showed two figures, kneeling and grasping each other in a massive hug, their faces buried in one another's shoulders. The title of the work was incidentally the old name of the church destroyed by Communism and rebuilt for the new Berlin, *"Versohnung"*, that is, "Reconciliation".

WEBS

When the light from the match glowed, I chanced to see the web stretched across the window's corner.

The man passing the restaurant window had paused, lit his cigarette, then faded into the darkness.

Since I knew the web was there, I'd glance up from my dinner and look at it every now and then,

Finding in its construction a measure of transcendent beauty.

Remarkably, the street lamp across the square, where the figure waited, backlit the web.

The more industrious the spider, the more visibly agitated the figure waiting.

At last, the man who lit the cigarette met the man beneath the lamp.

At that very moment, a moth landed on the web and was pierced by the waiting spider.

I pressed a silent alarm, and the uniforms moved in.

ALL EARS

An old poster from World War II reads: "Loose Lips Sink Ships." This vision of sailors at war drowning at sea should remain a powerful reminder that security begins with each one of us.

Today, many of us tend to think such concerns are outdated - ripe for the museum. We hear about economic espionage and our eyes glaze over. Do we really believe such a threat can compromise our survival? We should.

CONSIDER THE FOLLOWING:

Soldiers deployed around the globe can't afford to be compromised, and so we equip them with the means to dominate any battlefield. While this abstract idea may mean little to the average listener, try to personalize it.

What if your son or daughter depended on you to keep them alive? You would do everything in your power. But first, you would have to be fully informed about the threats they face. And so it is with espionage.

AGE OF ABUNDANCE

Espionage today is hardly like we once knew it. For the most part, researchers make up today's "spies." Yesterday's spy was equipped with poison pens and secret cameras. Today's collector is equipped with a laptop computer and modem, and a current library card.

These new information gatherers review databanks, technical journals and open publications for profit. They look for indications of new ideas, trends or conditions that may affect their own countries in some way. And they don't need to steal what they can already get their hands on free of charge.

Armed with this basic knowledge, these spies set about to gather specifics. They look for specific people with specific information. Aware that most North Americans protect classified information, modern spies look for items that are still "on the drawing board," which can be acquired before a classification stamp is put on.

Being a patient person, the modern collector then listens - to open phones, open faxes, open computers and after-hours discussions. We love to talk. We tend to be active, while the collector can be passive. He knows the North American trait of impatience with methodological security measures will ultimately betray us. He simply has to wait for us to talk about classified information in open restaurants, on planes and especially on the phone.

LANDS OF ORIGIN

You'll notice I haven't mentioned which country this new collector represents. The reality is that these people may simply represent another company - your competition. Economic advisors openly advertise in newspapers on ways to get a jump on our competitors. The ideas range from soliciting information for payment from enterprising or disgruntled employees to eliciting information at conferences open to the general public.

What is the best defense against this new method of economic voyeurism? Know what you must protect.

Prior to any joint meetings, have your team discuss what will and will not be discussed, and stick to it. Check documents for content before you publish them. And assume that if you say something out in the open, the information is compromised.

There's enough proof in the field today to show that there is no safe, open means of communication. The spies of the 21st century won't break the laws if they don't have to. They'll just listen.

REGULAR JOE

I'm wary of heroes. As for those who proclaim their values too self-righteously, I avoid them. Reality seldom matches legend. When asked to put their name on ethics standards, few participate. One reason for my reluctance to be swept along in any cause is because no one, and no mission, is above reproach. There is no greatest generation, just as there is no lost generation. The great writer Joseph Conrad knew the heart of darkness beats within each of us. That's why our real personality may only come through when tested. Will we do right, or wrong? Do we believe everyone has a dignity to be respected, or not? What will we stand for, or even die for? This story happened in Vietnam.

From the air, Vietnam looked verdant, even inviting. As the helicopter neared the ground, the parched farm fields spread out in every direction. All was silent, except for the white noise of the internal radio headsets. A warrant officer in intelligence, Joe was to be attached to an infantry company already deployed into this humid, suffocating, heat-ridden countryside. He could see the Americans below. As the rotors adjusted into a hover, he saw the soldiers surrounding a crowd of cowering, screaming Vietnamese farm folk.

Before getting out, Joe said to the pilot, "Wait for me a minute until I give you the high sign." Nodding in agreement, the pilot kept the helicopter running after Joe hopped out, and walked over to the tumult of people surrounded by edgy soldiers.

Assessing the scene of chaos before him, Joe shouted above the pandemonium, "What's going on here?" He couldn't hear what the soldiers shouted or answered, but clearly heard the red-faced lieutenant who ran up to him call out, "What are you doing here? You don't know what's going on around here!"

"I know what you guys are doing. Just stop. Let them go." Joe recalled that the whole scene happened so quickly, he didn't realize how afraid he was. All he remembered was the roiling crowd in front of him; that they didn't stop screaming while his exchange with the lieutenant continued.

"Just get back on that helicopter and get out of here!" screamed the young officer.

With that, Joe walked from near the helicopter, and stood between the Vietnamese and the US Army soldiers aiming at them. At that point, they were aiming at him, too. At that moment as well, Joe described terror.

He was never so afraid for his life in a career in the service, staring at young American soldiers aiming directly at his face and chest.

Joe just stood there, and didn't say a word. The Huey helicopter shook; the Vietnamese behind him bellowed and howled, and the now silent GIs, cocked and loaded in front of him, drew his measure.

Terror. Joe knew terror.

How long he was there, he couldn't say. The pilot watched from behind non-reflective headgear, his craft still running. The soldiers were large men with rifles; he recalled not one single face. The lieutenant could have been the furious head of a firing squad.

At last, a lieutenant shouted, "Men! Toward the tree line, move out." And then it was over.

When I read about heroes, I think about Joe. Joe is a quiet man, and would never be one you'd look at twice in a crowd. He could be anyone with life-long values, values he quite literally stood for in a field so long ago in Vietnam. No cause, and no mission, is worth the loss of your soul.

SECRET CONSTRUCTION

Huge tunnels were bored into the Harz Mountains at a place called Dora-Mittelbau, Germany. They were to protect the Nazis' V-2 rocket plant from Allied bombers. The tunnels were also the site of mass murder. To build the rockets, most estimates conclude 20,000 slaves from across Europe were tortured, beaten, and worked to death there. Strangely, some sixty years after the last SS guard ran away from the advancing US Army, Dora's legacy comes to directly affect Huntsville, Alabama.

A seminar at the University of Alabama, Huntsville, is entitled "Dora and the V-2, Slave Labor and the Space Age". It notes an inexplicable reality. Huntsville, the Rocket City, earned its title due to Project Paperclip, which brought captured German rocket scientists to America. They developed our rocket program which resulted in the magnificent trip to the moon and back. For this grand accomplishment humanity will honor them forever.

And yet, is this fair? Is it fair to commemorate men who knowingly used slave labor to produce their first rockets, then brought that science to America? Otherwise stated, is it fair to forget those who were beaten to death, often with sticks and boots like rabid animals, in the production of those flying Nazi bombs?

Photographs at the Huntsville University Library show dramatic scenes. Some were captured on scraps of paper by those who risked their lives to do so. They reveal beastliness, brutal, inhuman conditions, and macabre death scenes. One scene freezes forever the hanging of several prisoners, their mouths locked shut by sticks and cords. These devices were to prevent them calling out to the assembled slaves, arrayed to see the sight, and tremble.

Slavery. We in this country fought a civil war to end that stain. One speaker at the conference said no memorial should only mourn the dead. No, a democracy's strength is how it can objectively face its past, the better to learn from it. How can we do less in our city? If, due to the horrible death of so many others, our future as the center for space travel began, surely we can acknowledge that fact.

Our Space and Rocket Museum should have a permanent display, perhaps using some of those photos or items on display at UAH. Our city's Big Spring Park, or Von Braun Center, could memorialize those murdered Europeans. UAH could commemorate them, the better to remind young engineers of the future that life's choices have consequences. Science affects the lives of people, not just equipment. We should, after all, have an ethical awareness of cause and effect. This awareness should inform our actions. We should concretely recognize that while we did not cause the murders, indeed were the liberators of the slaves, we must do more.

We can honor those murdered by Hitler. Their slave labor led not only to the development of Hitler's weapons of vengeance, but gave us the basis of those wonderful ships which took us to the moon. The world needs to know that these dead too, were as one professor observed, "Rocket Men." Also, as so poignantly observed by one panelist, such recognition would wring immeasurable good out of unspeakable evil. The great German poet, J. C. Friedrich Hölderlin said as much when he wrote "Near, but difficult to grasp, the God. But where there is danger, the saving powers also rise." The thousands murdered, those denied every single dignity in the great danger that was Dora, might finally receive an earthly dignity. We of Huntsville have only to recognize them in this, our Rocket City.

DECEPTION *MAGIC!*

German bombers rumble relentlessly across the night sky of North Africa following a radio beam directed from German-occupied Libya toward the British port of Alexandria, Egypt. The flight commander notes an anomaly. The beam directs him forward, but he can see the lights of Alexandria to his left. The beam is known to be correct, but below him are city lights. Not only can he see the few inevitable lights in violation of blackout, he can easily see ships' lights in the harbor. He turns toward the lights and bombs . . . nothing.

In Africa during World War II, German bombers were led astray by an English deception plan that included mimicking Alexandria harbor. Creating the illusion of the actual city, lit by false house and ship lights, British officer Jasper Maskelyne, a professional magician, deceived the deadly German bombers into dropping their bombs eight miles from Alexandria.

Deception on the battlefield is a force multiplier whose target is the adversary's mind as much as his technology. Deception can be countered by understanding the rules that govern suggestion or, better said, magic.

Successful deception events are occurring worldwide. Despite being monitored by sophisticated surveillance techniques and technology, India exploded a nuclear device under the world's nose. In Kosovo, the Serbs used fake tanks to drain away allied air sorties. Artillery that the Vietnamese "did not have" at Dien Bien Phu appeared as if by magic after having been secretly delivered from the Korean peninsula. In each case, the adversary was well and truly deceived.

Appearance, Belief, Enticement

The great Chinese military philosopher Sun Tzu wrote, "All war is deception. Hence, when able to attack, we must seem unable. . . . When we are near, we must make the enemy believe that we are far way. [We must] hold out baits to entice the enemy." Almost every U.S. Army officer has read Sun Tzu's words. Yet, the U.S. military is little prepared for deception operations, which comprise a significant component of information operations. Why?

U.S. analysts tend to misinterpret Sun Tzu's text. Americans are a pragmatic, formulaic, and technology-trusting people. Sun Tzu uses verbs that refer to the mind, emphasizing appearance, belief, and enticement. How something seems or appears, what is believed, and enticement are activities discerned by the mind, not by technology. Deception in war deceives first the mind, then the eye. Few U.S. military analysts would dispute this, but fewer still offer assessments as if they believe it.

Basic military intelligence apparatus is sensory. We use platforms to see and hear the enemy. We base assessments on what is perceived as cold, rational fact. Appearance, belief, and enticement are mental, not sensory words. The U.S. military interprets enemy activities based on what can be seen, heard, and touched.

When a weaker country confronts a great power, the weaker knows it must employ deception to prevail. The U.S. Army's lack of ability in recognizing deception makes it not only vulnerable but also weaker because deception is a force multiplier.

The principles of magic, which all of us-especially children-enjoy, include the following:
- Disappearance.
- Appearance.
- Transposition of objects.
- Physical change in an object.
- Apparent defiance of natural law.

- Invisible sources of motion.
- Mental phenomena.

These principles also govern deception. We all know the old adage that the hand is quicker than the eye. The magician seems to deceive the eye, but this is not true. The hand is not quicker than the eye. The magician actually beguiles the eye. In war, an opponent tries to beguile his adversary's perception. What appears factual might actually be an artful creation with which to convince the adversary that it is real. Properly understood, these principles can be used to assess the battlefield, to assess intelligence reports, and to defeat deception attempts.

Deceiving the Mind

Before the enemy employs deception, he must analyze the situation, because to defeat his enemy, he must first understand how the enemy thinks. He can then orchestrate the adversary's responses. He will work to understand the enemy better than the enemy understands himself, then he will deceive the enemy's brain, not his eye.

The **Germans v. the Soviets**. Soviet dictator Joseph Stalin despised and feared English Prime Minister Winston Churchill more than he did German dictator Adolf Hitler. Indeed, we know that in 1941 Stalin believed that reports of an imminent German attack were part of a brilliant British disinformation campaign, not a brilliant German deception operation. Even when undeniable Wehrmacht military buildups were observed and reported by Communist spies, Stalin dismissed the reports because the Germans had orchestrated an illusion that played to Stalin's fears of the British.

The Germans suggested that the buildups were simply to pressure the Soviets for concessions in an upcoming parlay, making Stalin believe the buildups were in no way a prelude to war. In fact, when a German diplomat stated that war was imminent, Stalin believed and asserted that the nefarious disinformation had reached the ambassadorial level. The Germans had only to convince Stalin of their benign intent until they were ready to launch the great assault of Operation Barbarossa.

In World War II, during the battle of Stalingrad, massed Soviet gunfire suppressed German artillery batteries one by one. Even when the Germans were out of sight, crater analysis served Red Army intelligence sufficiently well to blast enemy gunners. Except for one battery, the German guns were silenced. This unseen battery fired away, despite massive counter-battery fire.

Soviet analysts plotted and targeted every meter of ground near where the guns could possibly be. Yet the Germans kept firing and killing Russians by the score. The mystery was only solved after the Germans surrendered. The wily battery commander had hammered his guns into the frozen Vistula River. Thus, he appeared to be defying natural law. The facts did not change; the enemy's brain had been tricked.

'Nordpol' was the code name of a German deception operation practiced against Great Britain early in World War II. British-trained agents were dropped into Holland from secret night flights. Each agent had a radio with which to contact London to vouch for his safe arrival and subsequent actions. Despite the fact that when reports began to come in they did not include confirmation codes, the British never suspected that the operation was compromised. Only when one of the imprisoned British agents escaped was the truth revealed.

Desire to believe something is true can cause the denial of confirmatory observations. In this case it was often believed that the agents were too tired or too mentally drained to identify themselves properly. The allies ascribed reasons to each and every inaccurate message. The Germans gave just enough true information to offset any total reassessment by the British agents. Thus, a subtle form of disappearance was used. The absence of confirmatory codes was explained away by simply allowing the British to fill in the reason themselves. After all, were not valid, if relatively insignificant, messages coming from the agents on the ground?

German counterintelligence personnel knew that a deception must fool the prevailing adversarial interpretive mind. They understood that when bureaucracies vouch for something, they are virtually impervious to change thereafter. When the first captured British-trained agent's confirmation was believed by his English handlers, the Germans concluded the others would be also. The Germans knew that the most difficult path for any analyst was to try to counter received opinion, particularly in the intelligence field. If the high command said all was well, who were the analysts to argue?

The **Arabs v. the United States**. The Arab world regularly denounces the U.S. media's stereotypical portrayal of its inhabitants as Middle Eastern terrorists. Osama bin-Laden exploited this situation when, instead of attacking embassies in the Middle East, his followers blew up two U.S. embassies in Africa, where the attack was a total surprise. The sudden appearance of Arab terrorists in benign backwater countries far from disputed areas was something the United States had never suspected or planned for.

The **Russians v. the Chechens**. During the recent Chechen rebellion against Russia, the Russians trapped Chechen rebels in Grozny. The rebels offered the Russians hundreds of thousands of dollars to allow Chechen fighters to escape safely through a minefield that surrounded the beleaguered city. The Chechens knew Russian corruption well. In fact, they had bought many weapons and much ammunition from the Russians for money and hashish. Why not pay to survive to be able to fight another day?

The money was passed, the path through the minefield was cleared, and the day of escape approached. At dawn, the Chechens entered the minefield. To their shock, the Russians, using registered artillery fire, began firing on the Chechens, forcing them to run in panic into areas where the mines had not been cleared. A Russian general commented later that what surprised him was that the Chechens believed the Russians at all.

Chechen perception of what was true about individual mercenary practices was not true about the Russians' relentless will as a group. Russian individual corruption could not be extrapolated to the entire army. We can learn from this that we can be deceived by our own preconceptions when falsely applied to known facts.

WHAT THE MIND BELIEVES

Many people still debate whether British and American double agents Kim Philby and Alger Hiss were actually guilty of spying for the enemy. They were of a certain social class, therefore many people consider the possibility that they could have been traitors inconceivable. If all members of a leading social class are loyal, how can they betray their country? The trick was observable, but the mind did not want to believe. Even when Hiss appeared in the Venona decrypts, his supporters refused to believe he was guilty. If Philby and Hiss were guilty, a Veritàble "natural law" was compromised.

During World War II before the attack at El Alamein in North Africa, the British were confronted with the problem of how to hide thousands of barrels of gasoline. The solution was to line the barrels up side by side, snug against the edge of abandoned trenches that had been dug months earlier. The German analyst, having viewed the same trenches in dozens of aerial photos, would not notice that the trench shadow was just a little wider than before. What appeared to be truck parks with lazy campfires nearby confirmed for the analyst the absence of danger. Yet, when the British attacked, it was with well-fueled tanks that had been hidden under fiberboard truck covers. The attack turned the tide in the Sahara in favor of the British. Trans-position of objects helped defeat German aerial observers because although they observed the field of battle, they never really saw it.

During World War I, when the Arabs revolted against the Turks, British military liaison T.E. Lawrence and Arabian tribesmen appeared to be mired in a torpid, sleepy wadi, unable to take a major town or, indeed, to even formulate a plan. Suddenly Lawrence and his compatriots struck as if from nowhere to take the town of Aqaba. The Turks were shocked because they believed that the wide, sandy wastes could not be crossed.

In World War II, U.S. General Douglas MacArthur believed the Chinese army incapable of advance without detection by the United States' superior aerial intelligence systems. Chinese General Mao Zedong's army advanced by night, using the threat of death to keep the men under cover by day. They took U.S. troops by surprise by secretly crossing the Yalu.

Appeared (seemed), believed, enticed; these are abstract words; words of the mind, not of technology. U.S. analysts must be aware of preconceptions. They must ask themselves what they believe to be true. This is perhaps the hardest question they can ask themselves. Whoever answers this question will best be able to use, or defeat, deception. This casts into high relief what Sun Tzu meant when he said, "If you know the enemy and know yourself, you need not fear a hundred battles."

Exploiting Beliefs

If we know ourselves, we have identified the first target of an adversary's deception. We can then ask how the enemy might try to deceive us. What is he doing to exploit our beliefs? What is he doing to make us believe something? How is he making himself appear? What will he try to entice us into doing? Using these concepts to manipulate us can be powerful force multipliers to a determined enemy.

If we apply counter deception, which corresponds to an awareness of the principles of suggestion as used in magic, we can begin to interpret an adversary's schemes. The power of suggestion, or magic, has been used for thousands of years. The old adage, "we are not deceived; we deceive ourselves," is only true if we allow it to be

UNDERCOVER

Dedicated to all those who live in undercover roles among the enemy.

Would you do it?

And at what price?

He lived among the most dangerous of people; can you really know what that means?

Oh, and there was no way out, if they found out who he was. There was no appeal, no lawyer, because they followed no law.

This was a one way street. Dare we say, victory or death?

Imagine the worst, then imagine something beyond that, because your captors can.

Would you do it?

And at what price?

CONFIDENCE DISPELS FEAR

Always ask questions, especially if everything makes sense. Who is the man sitting on the train across from you?

Why is the woman at the restaurant only paying in cash?

Why does the clock appear to have two men intently watching it?

You begin to see them all as reflections of yourself.

Confidence dispels apparent fear. Is it real, or feigned?

Do they belong where they are? Do you?

Do they have any relationship with what is going on around you?

Has that man been replaced by another?

Act as if you belong where you are. Confidence dispels fear.

THE LIVES OF OTHERS

Throughout the Cold War, a relentless barrier of concrete, barbed wire, vicious dogs, machine guns, mines and guard towers, which ran the width of Europe, separated the Western allies from the Soviet Bloc. Early in my military career, I spent time at the Berlin Wall and along the Inner-German Border, or Iron Curtain. There I only saw my enemy through binoculars, or as a gray presence far away. It was only years and years later, as a middle-aged man, that I was given the chance to see them as they saw themselves, in the remarkable German movie, "The Lives of Others." For that revelation, I have to thank the quiet star of that film, Ulrich Mühe.

In a strange way I believe I know Ulrich Mühe. He is the great German actor whose stellar career was capped when he won personal, international honors for his role as the Secret East German State Security, or 'Stasi', officer in "The Lives of Others". This German production won the Oscar for best foreign film in 2007. In this movie he portrayed with uncanny clarity the inner turmoil of a true believing Communist security officer whose society, decayed from within, employs his secret skills to elicit information from an entourage of literary and artistic fellow citizens. When he learns he serves only his masters' personal aims, rather than those of the national security, he gradually rebels at the hypocrisy and corruption. He truly portrayed a conscience in turmoil.

Mühe was born in a little town named Grimma, in what was once the Communist East 'German Democratic Republic' district of Saxony. He was only a few months younger than me. He became a construction worker out of school, then performed his national service as a guard at the Berlin Wall, or as the Communists would have called it then, the "anti-fascist protection wall". I believe that it was there, while doing his duty at the wall, he changed. I know it changed me.

In 1977, as a young artillery officer, I saw the Iron Curtain for the first time. It impressed me, raised in St. Louis, Missouri, so much so that upon my return I reflected upon that modern barrier:

"Westminster College, Missouri, is an ocean and a continent away from Hof, West Germany. What they have in common is the Iron Curtain. Winston Churchill coined the phrase at Westminster during a commencement exercise. Graduates of that day over 30 years ago can still see the subject of his address if they were to visit Hof, a post of the US Army in Bavaria.

A tour of the inner-German border is conducted there by members of an American armored cavalry regiment. The tour is somber, with undertones of a bazaar side show. Held behind a relentless apparatus of steel, concrete, dogs, machine-guns, soldiers, and landmines is the 'new socialist society'. As far as the eye can see, the fence complex reaches across town, fields and hills. But people built the thing.

I imagine macabre East German engineering awards distributed for wall innovations. Here a stipend for self-firing devices activated by a person attempting to scale the wall. There professional recognition for the creator of the iron bar that can stop 32 tons of pressure. Who could this be? Why?

The permanence of the fortified border is more psychological than physical. No construction expense is too great to impede a new escape technique, but in the end, the mind is the greatest deterrent to escape. Each two million Deutsch Mark kilometer of barrier is supported by a Communist miasma of half-truths and lies. Together they serve to keep the people in a constant atmosphere of distrust. Distrust is rewarded in that strange land. The armed apostles of the new socialist faith always travel in pairs, one to prevent the other from escaping. Who will report me? Who will report my plans? These are the questions that stop escapes, more so than barbed wire, dogs and mines.

'Go ahead, Comrade, escape to the West. We still have the wife and kids.' This cynical choice is a fact of East German life. This is what passes for a modern 20th century civilized nation. Hostage taking was outlawed by Pope Innocent III in another age, termed dark.

In a field not far from Hof, a balloon carrying two escaping East German families landed. These families will always hold a special place with me in the years to come when I remember Hof. They are free now, just as we are. They prove that even beyond the wall there will always be places where thoughts remain free."

I had no idea then that perhaps I was describing the turmoil really working upon the soul of the guard, Ulrich Mühe. For all I knew, he was literally one of the guards I saw 'over there' beyond the wall in the east. They were forbidden to wave at us, and had to hold the binoculars to their eyes whenever they looked across the border towards us in the West.

The miasma of distrust is what characterized that dictatorship. Mühe left his military service after his time at the wall and became an actor. He became an actor because he believed that at least in that profession, in that country, people spoke the truth to one another. Upon the collapse of the wall and the end of Communist East Germany in 1989, he learned differently. Given access to his Stasi files, he learned that not only four of his closest colleagues, but his very wife, were compelled to inform on him for years.

Wholly one out of every 14 people in the Stalinist East 'German Democratic Republic' were either willing or co-opted workers for the Secret security apparatus. Imagine the anguish of learning that those you trusted, those you loved, informed against you. Imagine then as they secretly confess to Communist agents about your political loyalties, your beliefs, and your every action. Imagine too that this wasn't enough. The Stasi were masters of the telephone tap, the hidden camera, the surveillance personnel, the faked encounter, the elicitation and the ultimate betrayal. This was life in a police state. This is when Ulrich Mühe finally said 'enough'.

Ulrich Mühe stood for all the cameras of the world in 1989, when it took great courage since the Communists had not yet given in, and spoke at Alexander Platz, the Times Square of old East Berlin. He denounced the Communist system, and demanded freedom of speech and freedom from police state oppression.

Thus, when in later years he portrayed someone living under that system, he was wholly prepared, indeed by his entire lifetime, to do so. He was quite literally born for that role. His characterization of what it meant to live in that place, in those times, will live forever. When asked about his success, it is said his response was, "I remember." Ulrich Mühe died of stomach cancer at the age of 54 only months after the "The Lives of Others" won the Oscar in 2007. He was born for his star, because he remembered, and told the truth. He helped me understand; he made me a better man.

SARAJEVO TALE

As I write this, bombs and rockets burst across the Middle East. Shrapnel and metal shards tear human flesh, never mind the age of the killed, blinded, or maimed. Somewhere a man is carefully aiming, firing, and recording whether he impacted his target or not.

This is our modern world. I recall a warm summer's day and a photograph handed me by a friend who just returned from reserve duty in Bosnia. The picture was a distance shot of embattled Sarajevo, city of untold horrors. Combat there tended toward the surreal. Snipers would use hunters' scopes to shoot high powered rifles from a hillside into the city, striking civilians running between blocks in their daily quest for food and water. When bored by these human carnival galleries, heavy artillery would open up on random targets, blasting ancient churches, synagogues and mosques of this once ecumenical city.

"Weren't you just there?" I asked my friend. "What is all this snow on the hillside?" A seeming crest of new fallen snow covered the mountains just beyond the buildings. The photo appeared a strangely beautiful cityscape. "That's not snow," he observed. "Those are tombstones."

A halo of war-wrought tombstones covered a city where the 1984 Winter Olympics were once held. Where sportsmen had competed and international tourists enjoyed life, machine guns spoke. Where once a genuine peace prevailed amidst shared cultures and mutual respect, ethnic mayhem ensued. Where even the Olympic Stadium's architecture held out hope for a holistic understanding of one another's culture and religion, high explosives fell. Instead of the growth of our common hopes for our children's' future, gunfire spat. Yet it was also from this doomed city of Sarajevo that another story came into my life, offering hope for our modern future. Peace can still triumph, and I witnessed this transformation myself. Seas of religious and ethnic blood are not Man's Fate. It doesn't have to be this way. Consider the story of Kurt.

Kurt crossed my life's path when I toured Antalya, Turkey, with my wife last summer. Kurt was middle aged, a fit and aware business-man and eye doctor; he was born in Sarajevo, Bosnia. As strangers who know they will probably not meet again in this world, we spoke freely about beliefs, children, and our hopes for our world. We hoped we could, by such dialogue, really be the bridge that stops conflict, to-day, in our own small ways. And perhaps, who knows, our world might then change in great ways. I remember mentioning a popular Ameri-can song which quoted a medieval Italian mystic, "Let there be peace on earth, and let it begin with me." Incidentally I mentioned that I was a soldier once, and had seen enough of death and hatred for a lifetime. Kurt said he was a soldier once, too. And then, on our way back to our hotel from a visit to a local family, Kurt, a man who till then had been a fine host, became a most remarkable witness to truth. He told his story to our small group in a swaying mini-van.

Kurt said, after some three and a half years as a soldier during the Yu-goslav civil war, "...a person becomes like an animal. He cares only about survival, and how to kill to stay alive. He doesn't care about any-thing, or anyone. One night I was told by my commander that five Turks had arrived within our lines in Sarajevo. They'd risked every-thing to come through enemy occupied country. It had taken them five days of clandestine travel to cover only a few kilometers, and were nearby. So I went to translate for them. I asked, 'Where are the arms for us?' and they answered they brought no weapons. I was incred-ibly angry at them, and said so. I asked in frustration why they risked their lives then to come to this city under direct artillery fire for noth-ing. They answered, 'To bring peace.' 'Peace?' I screamed, 'We need arms and ammunition!' 'We want to build a school', they answered. I laughed at them, and their naïveté. 'You know,' they said, 'one day this war will be over. And we want to build a school here for all children that teaches that war isn't the answer. Dialogue, tolerance for one an-other, and a good education will keep our children from doing to each other what we are doing now.' "

Kurt then said something I'll never forget; "I went back to my bunker that night, alone, frustrated, and raging. I cursed the Turks. I cursed God who seemed to have cursed us. The Turks came all that way, and brought no weapons with them for us at all. Almost the entire night passed over my fury and rage. Then suddenly I felt a powerful change, and I began to cry. A peace like I'd never known came over me. I experienced a great sorrow in my heart. I realized they were right, and I was wrong. What had I become in these three and a half years? Education, and love, would change the future, not guns. And that is how I came to believe in the principles of dialogue and tolerance."

The Turks were offered the totally leveled property where once stood a Sarajevo school. With money raised in a an All-Star international soccer tournament in Turkey, sponsored by a Turkish peace movement, they built their school. Today that school has one of the highest academic rankings in Bosnia; it is attended by diplomatic corps' children, and is open to all faiths. "That night in Sarajevo changed me. I became what God wanted." Kurt concluded. Kurt became a good Muslim, and a good man. He also became my friend.

A Rabbi on our trip who listened along with me stated simply, "A splendid man.